Bayou Plantation Country
COOKBOOK

Bayou Plantation Country
COOKBOOK

BY ANNE BUTLER

PELICAN PUBLISHING COMPANY
GRETNA 2006

The word "Pelican" and the depiction of a pelican are trademarks
of Pelican Publishing Company, Inc., and are registered in the
U.S. Patent and Trademark Office.

Library of Congress Cataloging-in-Publication Data

Butler, Anne, 1944-
   Bayou plantation country cookbook / by Anne Butler.
      p. cm.
   Includes index.
   ISBN-13: 978-1-58980-319-0 (hardcover : alk. paper)
   1. Cookery, American—Louisiana style. I. Title.
   TX715.2.L68H34 2006
   641.59763—dc22
                                        2006016909

Printed in China

Published by Pelican Publishing Company, Inc.
1000 Burmaster Street, Gretna, Louisiana 70053

Contents

Introction

They called the lower reaches of the Mississippi the "river of riches" for the fabulous wealth of the immense cotton and sugar plantations lining its banks, and they called Bayou Lafourche the "world's longest street" because of the elbow-to-elbow small Acadian farms that once stretched along its hundred-mile course from the river to the gulf. Both of these waterways were the most important transportation routes of their day, before railroads, before automobiles, really even before roads fought their way through the tangled undergrowth of this semitropical landscape.

Along these watery routes first came the slim, silent canoes, followed by the vessels of the earliest European explorers, then the flatboats that drifted with the current in only one direction so that the boatmen who wanted to return to where they'd launched had to hoof it home. Then arrived the floating river palaces called steamboats, with their opulent luxury and overheated boilers with a propensity for blowing the boats to smithereens midstream, often occasioning great loss of life. To the bayous came the shrimp trawlers and oyster luggers and fishing boats and the trappers' pirogues piled high with furs and push-poled through tight, shallow spots in the swamps. They shared the water with the smaller steamers that delivered the mail and the groceries and the schoolchildren and the news from dock to dock to dock up and down the bayou.

Property descriptions emphasized the valuable river or bayou frontage, where the land was richest and water access easiest. From the water the plantations and farms reached back in slender, fertile fingers in this felicitously warm climate. Water access was all important. It was the waterways that transported the early settlers and plantation families back and forth to the center of business and the lively social season in New Orleans. It was the waterways that transported the crops downriver to factors for sale to markets east and west, the steamboats sometimes so heavily laden with bales of cotton or hogsheads of sugar that only the smokestacks were visible above the load. It was also the waterways that transported back to the plantations and farms the fine furnishings and practical wares purchased by the sale of these crops, or at least by the credit extended.

Of course the waterways were fickle friends at best. Besides providing transportation and enriching the land with sediment, these same waterways swelled each spring with melting snow and heavy rains upriver, turning into raging torrents, bursting through crevasses in the tenuous levees to wipe out crops and homesteads alike. Planters along the Mississippi River and the distributary bayous in the 1800s were required to construct and maintain levees to protect their properties. Sometimes the levees held. Sometimes they did not, since some were just a few feet high, and the consequences were disastrous. In 1927 the most extensive flood in the history of the entire country left 26,000 square miles under water and more than 600,000 people homeless, huddled in Red Cross tent cities along the lower Mississippi.

The waters, both river and bayou, have had an enormous impact on the life along their banks, giving and taking, enriching and eroding from the days of Indian settlements through the French and Spanish colonial periods. The antebellum plantation culture spread up the river from New Orleans, then the country's busiest port, and downriver from Natchez.

The early indigo and cotton plantations gave way to sugar in this area after Etienne de Boré in 1795 improved the process for turning cane syrup into granulated sugar, and the introduction in 1817 of hardy ribbon cane improved its commercial viability. A free man of color born in New Orleans but educated in Paris, Norbert Rillieux in the 1830s developed the vacuum pan method of cooking the syrup, a technological advance that coupled with the advent of steam power for transportation and manufacturing fueled the expansion of the sugarcane culture and the potential for great profits.

Along the Mississippi River between Natchez and New Orleans lived the largest percentage of American millionaires in the 1850s. The riverbanks were lined with their splendid, columned mansions and immense plantations, with those of the West Bank maintaining much closer ties to the bayou than to New Orleans, since those were the days when crossing the river presented a major challenge. Along Bayou Lafourche the setting became much the same as the small farmers were pushed back from the richest lands along the bayou by the big planters.

There still remained enough small homesteads lining the bayou for that stretch to resemble one long neighborly street, and indeed Louisiana writer Harnett Kane, in his colorful manner, described the spreading of the news of the armistice ending World War I. Octave, at the northern end of the bayou, received the news in a telegram and jumped into his car to give the glad tidings to his cousin, way down at the other end of the bayou. When Octave started his car, however, his neighbor Arsene stuck his head out of his window to find out what was the matter, and Octave shouted, *"La guerre est finie!"* Arsene ran to his other window to call the news to Gustave in the next house down the bayou, who ran to his own window, and the exciting news traveled from house to house to house. When Octave finally reached by car the home of his cousin, the cousin rushed out first and cried, "Octave, you have heard? *La guerre est finie!"*

To the banks of the waterways came over the years settlers of many nations—the French, Spanish, English, Creoles, Africans, Germans, Italians, Acadians, not all of them arriving by choice—wresting their livelihoods from the rich lands along the river and bayou banks, sometimes amassing great masses of wealth, sometimes barely eking out enough to survive. Each nationality left its mark on the culture, architecture, economy, cuisine, language, traditions, and society, with adaptations for the local climate and the peculiar requirements of this particular place in history. These unique cultures ebbed and flowed with the times and the tides, coming and going, building and eroding, absorbing the enriching influences of other immigrant groups just as the riverbanks and wetlands of south Louisiana absorbed the sediments washed down from the watershed of the Ohio Valley and turned them into something distinctly different.

This rich blending of diverse influences, this cultural gumbo, this shifting, changing, seething life, this is south Louisiana's fascinating Bayou Plantation Country. Life is different here, always has been, along the West Bank of the Mississippi River and all along Bayou Lafourche to the coast. And as life is different here, so is the cooking. *Vive la difference!* Enjoy!

Bayou Plantation Country

COOKBOOK

Lower Louisiana Highway One

Louisiana's longest and oldest highway, LA 1, crosses from the northwestern corner of the state through the central part and then roughly parallels the Mississippi River from Lettsworth down past Port Allen to Donaldsonville, where it branches off to follow Bayou Lafourche on its meandering course to the coast at Grand Isle. Across the river from Baton Rouge, going south, LA 1 seems like a tiny ribbon floating in a sea of sugarcane, with endless fields stretching from each side of the roadbed. The state boasts nearly 600,000 acres of sugarcane, producing almost a fourth of the nation's sugar crop, and when traveling down LA 1, it seems that an enormous percentage of that crop can be seen from this very roadway. Indeed, a whole lot of it can.

Approaching Baton Rouge from the north, LA 1 bisects orderly rows of tall, stately sugarcane in flat fields stretching to the horizon as far as the eye can see, a vision broken only by intermittent clumps of trees, shaded spots where once were located the impressive homes of the early planters, and where a few of these old homes still stand. Then the road closely parallels Bayou Lafourche as it flows south to the gulf, passing lush vegetable gardens on the fertile grounds atop the batture, heavily laden citrus trees flourishing in the flood-enriched soil, and ancient live oaks whose graceful branches arch and dip down to the very ground.

Shrimp boats take the place of sugarcane bordering the lower stretch of LA 1 as solid ground gives way to shifting swamps and marshland, the

narrow 2-lane roadway in some places so slightly elevated above sea level that it floods during hurricanes. The low-lying road has traditionally posed a nightmare for mandatory evacuations, which must be ordered well in advance of landfall for seasonal visitors to the coastal resort of Grand Isle, as well as for the year-round residents of southern Lafourche and Jefferson Parishes and some 6,000 offshore oil workers who all must use the road to flee the storm, many pulling big boats behind them.

U.S. transportation secretary Norman Mineta, without undue exaggeration, called the lower section of the highway "a two-lane road that floods at the sight of rain." It is certainly no wonder that plans are underway for a new elevated roadway from Port Fourchon inland, but the new road won't come close to the fascination of the old. The new road will be safer. The new road will be faster. But match the charm and interest of old LA 1, called the longest street in the world? Never!

The main route of travel long before any highway was built, Bayou Lafourche was originally a tributary or distributary of the Mississippi River, *la fourche* meaning the fork in the river's flow. When the Mississippi River ran low, the entrance to Bayou Lafourche at Donaldsonville was so shallow it could be navigated at the mouth only by small boats, and even those often had to be towed over the bar by mule teams. But when the Mississippi was at flood stage, the high water turned Bayou Lafourche into a terrible torrent, sending swirling floodwaters through crevasses or breaks in the levees to swamp agricultural fields and wash away the rustic dwellings of the fishermen, trappers, and farmers clustered along the waterway.

The improved river levee system in 1904 cut the bayou off from the Mississippi, and its size and navigability at the upper end shrank accordingly. Steamboats used to dock on the bayou at the Madewood Plantation landing near Napoleonville when the bayou was 5 times broader than it is now. At present a pumping plant at Donaldsonville allows some water to enter the bayou from the river, and plans are being floated to reintroduce more of the Mississippi's waters into Bayou Lafourche. The plugging of the bayou takes a large share of the blame for land loss in the Barataria and Terrebonne basin wetlands, and it is hoped that diverting more sediment-rich river water down the bayou will increase land build-up and help slow coastal erosion.

Today, Bayou Lafourche flows right through the center of small communities. And that's right where the bayou should be, right in the center of things. The bayou has traditionally been the focus of these communities, for it was the source of food, the source of transportation, the source of livelihood, the very source of life. In many cases, it still is.

Shrimp trawlers and oyster luggers are tied up alongside the main road, along with all manner of other vessels: big boats, small boats, freshly painted boats painstakingly readied for yet another season of fishing and gleaming in the sun, older boats worn and weather-beaten by decades of battering by wind and waves. Each boat has its own special name, some more picturesque than others, many proudly proclaiming the port of origin.

A trip along LA 1 is a fascinating glimpse into Louisiana's all-important seafood industry and its vital importance to the life, culture, and economics of so many bayou families. First thing's first, though:

car traffic comes to a halt as bridges lift to allow the all-important boat traffic to pass.

Louisiana writer Harnett Kane said with his customary descriptive flair that the lands along Bayou Lafourche became "fragrantly French" in the late 1700s, when they received an influx of Acadians ousted from Canada in one of the British government's less-honorable moves, wrenched from their families and homes and flung to the far corners of the globe until a number of them managed to reunite in Louisiana's bayou country, where the language was familiar and the possibilities for living off the land seemed endless. Simple country folk, Kane called them, making the best of things in their tiny cottages with bousillage walls of mud and moss, exterior stairs climbing from the front gallery, rustic picket fences enclosing the small patches of property, asking little beyond "a lil land, a lil wife, a lot of chirren." Since most of the rich alluvial lands along the Mississippi close to New Orleans were held by the big Creole families with their aristocratic European backgrounds, the Acadians lived content along Bayou Lafourche, at least until the Americans moved in and the plantation culture with its big landholdings and its fancy mansions and its slaves and its wealth and its grasping hunger for expansion pushed many of the small farmers farther into the swamps and the marshes.

Along old LA 1 and Bayou Lafourche, even today, vestiges of both cultures are visible around every bend. Just as it's always "five o'clock somewhere," it's always festival time in one of these fun-loving little communities along the bayou, and that's the perfect time for visitors to enjoy the indigenous cooking. If there's one thing Cajuns like to do as well as eat, it's pass a good time, but who can separate the two? So join the locals at whatever festival is filling the air with the sounds of fiddle and accordion and the sizzle of sausage in a black-iron skillet. Go to as many as you can, because there's a festival celebrating just about everything you can eat around here, from oysters and shrimp to jambalaya, catfish, crawfish, boudin, you name it.

In this fascinating stretch of bayou plantation country, behind every door, whether the door is an immense mahogany one with stained glass sidelights or a rough unplaned cypress one with knotholes and rusty hinges, is a fabulous cook. That cook is just as likely to be male as female in this land where little boys at an early age learn to whip up sensational sauce piquantes and jambalayas in that usually all-male domain called the hunting camp. That cook, more than likely, is using recipes, whether written or remembered, that blend and meld many influences, all mixed to perfection with the seasonings and spices that make life so interesting in south Louisiana.

And that cook has an inborn instinct for harvesting the bounty of the bayou and the marshland, the gulf waters and the swamps. Think all those plastic jugs bobbing in the brown bayou waters are just so much floating debris? Think again, and while you're thinking, notice that those plastic jugs aren't going anywhere. That's because they are anchored in place to mark the location of crab traps, and many a meal is made from this bounty of the bayou. Here are a few favorite recipes for fresh crab.

Crabmeat Mousse

1-2 pkg. unflavored gelatin (1 or 2 tbsp.)
3-5 tbsp. dry sherry (cold water or chicken broth may be substituted)
1 clove garlic, finely chopped (optional)
2 3-oz. pkg. Philadelphia cream cheese
3 oz. blue cheese
1 can condensed cream of mushroom soup
1 cup onion, chopped (or substitute chopped green onions or shallots)
1 cup celery, finely chopped
2 tbsp. minced capers
Tabasco to taste
Seasoned salt or Herbamare to taste
1 cup mayonnaise
18 oz. fresh crabmeat, or 3 6-oz. cans white crabmeat, drained
Lemon juice to taste

Dissolve gelatin in sherry (or water or broth). Reserve. Add garlic to the cream cheese. In top of double boiler (or in casserole dish) on very low heat, warm the cream cheese and blue cheese with mushroom soup, stirring constantly until mixture is soupy. Add the softened gelatin. Stir to melt and thoroughly mix. Stir in onions and celery. Remove from fire. Add capers, Tabasco, and seasoned salt to taste, stirring thoroughly. Add mayonnaise. Stir thoroughly. Mix in crabmeat seasoned with lemon juice. Spray mold with non-stick oil spray. Put mixture into mold. Refrigerate overnight. Unmold and serve with party crackers. Serves 8-10.
Recipe from Judge Ian Claiborne.

Crab Dip

1 stick butter or margarine
1 bunch green onions, chopped
1 8-oz. pkg. cream cheese
1 tbsp. lemon juice
Cayenne pepper to taste
Cajun seasonings to taste
8-12 oz. crabmeat

Sauté butter and onions until tender. Cut cream cheese into pieces and add; stir until melted. Season with lemon juice, pepper, or Cajun seasonings. Gently mix in crabmeat. Serve warm with toast or crackers. Serves 6-8.
Recipe from Becky Power.

Avocado-Shrimp Remoulade

1 cup mayonnaise
1 tbsp. onion, chopped
1 tbsp. celery, chopped
½ tbsp. parsley, chopped
2 tbsp. Creole mustard
1 tsp. paprika
1 tbsp. prepared horseradish
1 splash hot sauce
¼ cup olive oil
1 tbsp. vinegar
½ tsp. Worcestershire sauce
¼ tsp. salt
2 lb. shrimp, cooked and peeled
½-1 lb. lump crabmeat
4 avocados

Make sauce by mixing all ingredients except seafood and avocados. Best mixed in a food processor. Add seafood to sauce. Refrigerate for several hours to allow flavors to blend. When ready to serve, halve the avocados, place seafood on avocado, and top with desired amount of sauce. Garnish with small wedges of tomato. Serves 4-6.
Recipe from Laurie Walsh.

Crab and Corn Bisque

½ lb. butter
3 tbsp. flour
1 onion, chopped
1 quart milk
1 16-oz. can cream corn
1 can cream of potato soup
¼ tsp. cayenne pepper
1 pt. crabmeat
¼ lb. Swiss cheese, grated
2 tbsp. parsley, chopped
2 tbsp. green onions, chopped

Melt butter in heavy pot. Stir in flour until blended but not brown. Add onions. Cook over medium heat until onions soften, about 10 minutes. Add milk, corn, potato soup, and pepper. Simmer about 15 minutes. Stir in crabmeat, cheese, parsley, and green onions just before serving. Serves 6.

Baked Seafood Sauterne

⅓ cup dry white wine
Dash Tabasco
1 10½-oz. can cream of chicken soup
½ green onion, chopped
3 tbsp. parsley, chopped
1 cup shrimp, deveined
1 cup crabmeat
½ cup mushrooms, sliced
2 tbsp. butter, melted
1 cup bread or cracker crumbs
2 tbsp. Parmesan cheese
Dash dried dill

Stir wine and Tabasco into undiluted soup. Combine chopped onion, parsley, shrimp, crabmeat, and mushrooms with soup. Turn into shallow baking dish or individual baking shells. Sprinkle with topping made by combining melted butter with crumbs, Parmesan, and dill. Bake at 350 degrees until thoroughly heated and browned on top, about 20-25 minutes. Serve immediately. Serves 4-6.

Soft-Shell Crab Bywater

12 small to medium softshell crabs
1 pt. milk
Salt and pepper
Flour
Melted butter
Lemon to garnish
Parsley to garnish

Meuniere Sauce

1 cup butter
2 tbsp. green onions, finely chopped
2 tbsp. parsley, chopped
4 tbsp. lemon juice
½ tsp. salt
2 dashes each: Worcestershire, red pepper
      sauce, cayenne

Hollandaise Sauce

1 tbsp. lemon juice
1 tbsp. tarragon vinegar
4 egg yolks
2 dashes Tabasco
Pinch paprika
Salt to taste
1 cup melted butter

Clean crabs of deadmen, sandbag, eyes, and apron. Wash in cold water and pat dry with towel. Season well. Soak crabs in milk seasoned with salt and pepper. Then pat lightly with flour and brush with melted butter. Place in a slow broiler for about 15 minutes, until cooked to a light brown. Make sauces while crabs are cooking.

For the Meuniere Sauce, melt butter in saucepan and add one at a time green onions, parsley, lemon juice, salt, and other seasonings, stirring well after each addition.

In a double boiler, beat lemon juice and vinegar into egg yolks. Cook on low heat in top of double boiler, stirring constantly. Add Tabasco, paprika, and salt during cooking. Do not let water come to boil. Remove from heat when thickens. Add in warm melted butter a little at a time, beating constantly. If desired, return to heat to rethicken.

To serve Soft-Shell Crab Bywater, cover each plate with a thin layer of Meuniere Sauce. Pour Hollandaise Sauce in the center of the plate until it forms a circle slightly larger than the crabs. Place crabs in the Hollandaise. Garnish with lemon slices and parsley. Serves 8-12.
Recipe from Pat Walsh.

Poplar Grove Plantation

The exuberance of decoration might seem over the top elsewhere, but it's entirely fitting and right at home for the whimsical raised dwelling known as Poplar Grove Plantation. No ordinary house, Poplar Grove began life as "an Oriental-inspired pavilion" built for the 1884 World's Industrial and Cotton Centennial Exposition in New Orleans on the site of present-day Audubon Park. Called the Bankers' Pavilion, it was designed by noted architect Thomas Sully to reflect the growing Western interest in all things Oriental, which explains the carved dragons set in the gallery brackets, the pagoda-like roofline, and the screens of Eastlake spindles looking for all the world like an oversized Oriental counting abacus.

In 1886, the Bankers' Pavilion was purchased by New Orleans businessman Joseph Harris. He moved it in one piece some 200 miles up the Mississippi River by barge, then laboriously hauled it over the levee to its base just on the other side. There it was raised high (8 feet off the ground) on brick piers to catch the cooling breezes off the river. Poplar Grove remains today one of only a few dwellings along the Mississippi River situated directly beside the levee. Most of the other structures either have been washed away or moved back so that they are separated from the levee and river by roadbeds or other obstructions.

Joseph Harris asked a young cousin, Horace Wilkinson of Plaquemines Parish, to manage his

sugar plantation in West Baton Rouge Parish. Horace and his wife, Julia, settled at Poplar Grove as the first to live in the house they would soon purchase, a house 5 generations of their descendants would call home. Their great-granddaughter, Ann Wilkinson, now owns the house and lives there.

Shaded by immense cypress, palm, magnolia, cedar, and live oak trees, Poplar Grove is surrounded by 4 acres of lush gardens brimful of giant gingers, sweet olives, bananas, crepe myrtles, roses, camellias, and azaleas. The older parts of the gardens were designed by Theodore and Lou Bird Landry, famed for lovely curved and bordered flowerbeds. These earlier parts were perfectly complemented by areas landscaped later by Steele Burden, a well-known Baton Rouge landscape designer whose family property became the Rural Life Museum and Windrush Gardens. Mr. Burden is remembered for planting the multitude of live oaks on the verdant Louisiana State University campus in Baton Rouge.

At Poplar Grove, he used towering cypress trees to hide the "secret garden" to the north of the house. Just days before his death in 1995, he laid out the landscaping for what had been the chicken yard, insisting upon renovating the old chicken house for Ann Wilkinson's son Steele, who is Burden's namesake, since, as he said, "Every young man needs a place to get away from his mother." These were the last gardens designed by the creative Mr. Burden, and they show his sensitivity to the unique setting and his vast knowledge of indigenous plantings.

Fertilized by centuries of the Mississippi's floodwaters, the soils here are so rich that the garden plants as well as the sugarcane grow to enormous proportions in this tropical setting. The plants not only thrive, but they also live long and healthy lives, so that all parts of the gardens at Poplar Grove could be anchored to nineteenth-century specimens.

The shaded grounds and lush plantings provide the perfect backdrop for the main house, which is painted a wonderful shade of mauve trimmed in cream and blue and aubergine with just a dab of gold leaf for excitement and a sky-blue gallery ceiling to deter the dirt daubers. The exterior paint colors are ideal for showing the trim work to best advantage. They also serve to set the stage for an interior equally exuberant and colorful.

Double mahogany doors with spectacular woodwork bordering etched and stained glass panels open into a broad hallway flanked by 2 main rooms on each side, with twelve-foot ceilings and immense floor-to-ceiling windows set off by 60-pane blue-and-gold checkerboard stained glass. Furnishings are true to the period and appropriate to the time and architecture of the house, which 5th-generation owner-occupant Ann Wilkinson calls "Anglo-Japanesque, Oriental with a little English aesthetic." Some furnishings have been inherited from earlier generations, while others have been carefully selected to complement the unique setting. Wall coverings are appropriate to the period as well, showcasing Victorian, Oriental, or Egyptian revival styles. Art and document papers with design motifs in the parlor alone range from birds and cherry blossoms to sunflowers, willows, bamboo lattice, and an Oriental sun. Throughout the house, the room arrangements and furnishings exhibit a colorful flair entirely suited to this unusual structure.

Located just across the Mississippi River from

bustling Baton Rouge, Poplar Grove is so well insulated from the world by its lush surrounding plantings that it seems magically isolated from the rest of the world. "The gardens," Ann Wilkinson says, "envelope the place and protect the visitor from any unexpected intrusion. So many of the plantation homes can be seen from the road, but Poplar Grove cannot and so it comes as a complete surprise." Poplar Grove is listed on the National Register of Historic Places. It is also accessible to visitors, by advance arrangements, for group tours or meals and small weddings. For information, contact Ann Wilkinson, Poplar Grove Plantation, 3142 N. River Road, Port Allen, LA 70767; telephone 225-344-3913; e-mail wilkinson.ann@gmail.com; Web site www.poplargroveplantation.com.

For generations the Great River Road has been noted as the setting for the grand Greek Revival mansions of the wealthy sugarcane planters of the 1830s, 1840s, and 1850s: Oak Alley, Houmas House, immense Nottoway. An upsurge of interest in cultural and heritage tourism has opened the door for a renewed appreciation of other architectural styles and influences—earlier, later, or just plain different—and houses such as lovely Laura and Poplar Grove have come into their own. Poplar Grove stands today as a glorious tribute, not only to an exuberant owner who has furnished it with just the right exotic and romantic pieces, but also to the remarkable melange of cultural influences that make up Louisiana history and architecture.

Deciding on recipes to use for this book took Ann Wilkinson on a stroll down memory lane, she said, back to the days of picking up pecans in the surrounding pasturelands; horseback excursions to fill buckets with ripe dewberries growing along the ditch banks in the sugarcane fields, along the railroad tracks, or behind the levee in the batture along the Mississippi River; and trips to the long-time family camp at Grand Isle, where the catch of the day ended up on the dinner table in delectable fashion, usually prepared by Manuel Phillips, who cooked at the plantation boarding house during grinding season. The Wilkinson family had extensive landholdings in coastal Plaquemines Parish and kept a boat at Lake Hermitage by which they made their way to Grand Isle before LA 1 was built, passing along the way Wilkinson Canal, Wilkinson Bay, and Wilkinson Bayou. The Grand Isle camp slept 30 and survived many a hurricane since it was built in 1936. Ann's great-grandfather Horace Wilkinson was one of the founders of the Grand Isle Tarpon Rodeo.

Back home at Poplar Grove, Ann's mother, Ruth, always loved hosting small dinner parties, and one of her most popular offerings was her Lobster Thermidor, also good with crabmeat.

Lobster (or Crab) Thermidor

Meat of 1 lobster, boiled, or 1 pt. lump crabmeat
1 doz. large, fresh mushrooms, sliced
6 tbsp. butter
Dash paprika
Dash dry mustard
1 cup sherry, sauterne or dry white wine
4 tbsp. flour
2 cups cream
1 tsp. salt, or salt to taste
½ tsp. parsley, minced
4 tbsp. grated Parmesan cheese
Pimento
1 lemon

If using lobster, clean and break meat into small chunks, or use lump crabmeat. Cook fresh mushrooms in 2 tbsp. butter for a minute or two. Add paprika, mustard, and sherry. Heat to boiling. Melt remaining butter, blend in flour, add cream, and cook until thickened, stirring constantly. Season with salt. Add mushroom mixture, lobster or crabmeat, and parsley. Fill crab shells or shell-shaped ceramic dishes with mixture. Sprinkle with cheese. Garnish with a slice of lemon and a "cross" of pimento strips. Bake at 425 degrees for 15-20 minutes. Serves 4.
Recipe from Ruth Wilkinson.

Stuffed Artichoke

1 artichoke
½ cup Italian breadcrumbs
½ cup Romano cheese, grated
¼ cup dried or fresh parsley
Ground bay leaf to taste
Italian seasoning to taste
Oregano to taste
Celery flakes or celery salt to taste
Salt to taste
1 tsp. pureed onion
⅛ tsp. pureed garlic
¼ cup olive oil
1 tbsp. lemon juice
2 big dashes Tabasco
Worchestershire sauce to taste

Cut off bottom stem and top of artichoke flower. Turn artichoke upside down and press lightly on bottom to open leaves. Cut off tip of each leaf. Hull out the center. Mix dry ingredients and fill each leaf with dry mixture. Mix all liquid ingredients and dribble over stuffed leaves. Steam artichoke in a covered pot with a little water in the bottom for 45 minutes or longer until artichoke is tender. Do not let water completely boil out. Serves 1.
Recipe from Ruth Wilkinson.

Manuel's Oysters

½ stick butter
1 cup celery
¾ cup bell pepper
1 cup green onion
½ cup oil
4 tbsp. flour
3 dozen oysters with liquor
1 tsp. Tony Chachere's Creole Seasoning
½ tsp. salt, or salt to taste
Chopped parsley for garnish

Chop and sauté vegetables in butter, then puree. Make a dark roux with oil and flour. Add roux to pureed vegetables. Drain and reserve oyster liquor, then add liquor to vegetables and roux. If more liquid is necessary, add a little white wine or water. Simmer about 5 minutes. Add oysters and cook until oysters are barely curled. Serve on hard toast points, over rice, or in individual ramekins. Sprinkle with fresh chopped parsley when ready to serve. Serves 4.

Dewberry Cobbler

1½ sticks butter
4 full cups freshly picked and rinsed
    dewberries
¾ tsp. salt
¾ cup sugar
1½ cups flour
2 tsp. baking powder
½ cup milk
1 egg

Preheat oven to 375 degrees. Melt ½ stick butter (4 tbsp.). Pour into 8x11" or 2-qt. Pyrex casserole dish. Spread melted butter in bottom of dish and cover with berries. Mix ¼ tsp. salt and ¼ cup sugar. Sprinkle mixture over berries. Mix flour, baking powder, ½ cup sugar, and ½ tsp. salt in a bowl. In a separate bowl, combine milk and egg. Stir milk and egg mixture into flour mixture. Beat until batter is smooth. Pour batter over berries. Bake for 30 minutes until batter is golden. Serve hot. You can add ice cream or pour rich cream over the servings. Serves 4-6.

Nottoway Plantation

The largest antebellum plantation house extant in the South, enormous Nottoway overlooks the Mississippi River, a veritable white castle towering over the flat sugarcane fields surrounding it. Completed in 1859 after 6 years of planning and 4 years of construction, the plantation house was an unusual combination of Greek Revival architecture spiced with an Italianate influence not common along the Great River Road in antebellum days.

Sixty-four rooms, 200 windows, a doorway for each day of the year, 16 fireplaces, and 7 interior stairways are enclosed under the original slate roof, a staggering total of 53,000 square feet in all. Fine red cypress was milled on location for the bulk of the construction. The main hall is 20 feet across with 15-foot ceilings. The formal dining room measures 25 by 35 feet, and the fine plaster frieze work around its ceiling, a mixture of mud, clay, horsehair, and moss, highlights the camellias beloved by the original mistress of the house.

A side wing was built for the 7 daughters of the family. To the rear are kitchen areas and a wing built to house the 4 sons, who were removed to this garconniere upon reaching age 14 so as not to be bad influences on their delicate sisters. The main entrance is reached by stately curved stairs of granite blocks raised above a full brick basement. Galleries are lined with cast-iron balustrades, but the rails are of wood so as not to be too hot to the touch in summer or too cold to the touch in winter. Along one entire side is a curved double-galleried wing enclosing the famous white ballroom, where everything is white from floor to ceiling, with splendid Corinthian columns supporting triple arches and elaborate plaster frieze work.

Nottoway was built to house the large family of aristocratic planter John Hampden Randolph, son of Judge Peter Randolph, who had moved south

from Nottoway County, Virginia, when President Monroe appointed him judge of the Court of Error and Appeals of Mississippi. Upon his death, the judge's widow married into the family at Beech Woods Plantation in Louisiana, where John James Audubon's wife, Lucy, conducted a school for the daughters of neighborhood planters, including "Jane and Margaret Towles, Margaret Butler, the Misses Randolph, Miss Harbour and the Swazie girls," as noted in the artist's diary.

When Judge Peter Randolph died, his 19-year-old son, John Hampden, was one of the executors of his estate. Soon John was raising his own crops of cotton. He married Emily Jane Liddell and together they moved south to a tract of more fertile land along Bayou Goula, where they planted cotton until they could raise the capital to put in sugarcane. Eventually the family prospered sufficiently

to purchase 4 plantations of more than 7,000 acres along the Mississippi River and set about planning a suitable abode.

Thirteen plans were submitted by New Orleans architects in response to John Hampden Randolph's request for a grand structure unique among the River Road's many fine homes. Randolph chose the design of Henry Howard, and construction began. Innovative ideas were implemented: 26 built-in closets and indoor bathrooms with hot and cold running water fed by cisterns atop the roof. The real jewel of the house was the white ballroom with its triple arches, and it would be the setting of elegant weddings for all of the radiant Randolph girls except one who died young.

The Randolphs lived a gay life in their white castle, with balls and elaborate picnics, music lessons for the children taught by a German professor who made the rounds of the neighboring plantations, and all manner of elegant entertainments. John Hampden Randolph was an enthusiastic hunter, as were most of the men of his day, stalking big game like deer or bear and shooting partridge and woodcock in the surrounding fields and wild duck on the lakes and coastal marshlands. His daughter Cornelia's diary, written in 1903, at a time when writing was not considered a suitably respectable calling for a genteel young lady and hence published cleverly under the pseudonym of M. R. Ailenroc (Cornelia spelled backwards), recorded a recipe for roasted bear claw, given below.

The happy family life lasted for only a few years, until the Civil War erupted. John Hampden Randolph removed his slaves to Texas and grew cotton there to support the family, while his wife remained at Nottoway, sending the teenage daughters to safe havens elsewhere and keeping by her side only the younger children and a few servants to help meet their needs.

During one river skirmish federal gunboats fired on the house, but when a Union officer recognized Nottoway as a place he had visited before the war, he ordered the guns to cease firing, and the house sustained only minor damage. Emily Jane Randolph had fiercely faced the soldiers from her front gallery, a dagger tucked into her belt, determined to save her home from suffering the fate of many abandoned riverfront mansions that were looted or burned. When the firing became heavy, she took refuge with her children and slaves on the ground floor with its brick walls 4 feet thick. She was 45 and gave birth to her eleventh child that same year, 1862; her oldest son, Algernon Sidney, was killed at Vicksburg the following year.

The Randolphs reunited at war's end and remained at Nottoway for several decades. John Hampden died in 1883 and his grieving widow sold the property 6 years later for $100,000; its next transfer would be at a sheriff's sale for nonpayment of taxes. Nearly a century later, in 1980, it was purchased by preservationist Arlin Dease, who restored the home to its former glory and opened it to the public for daily tours, a tradition continued by present owner Paul Ramsay of Australia, who took over ownership in 1985.

On the National Register of Historic Places, Nottoway is a popular B&B as well as a spectacular setting for weddings and receptions, especially the white ballroom. Even today, the furnishings are elegant enough to echo the extravagance and ease of antebellum life there, with fine 4-poster beds, backless bustle chairs for the ladies to accommodate that particularly unbecoming fashion, sideless chairs to allow the swords of uniformed soldiers, and curtains in the gentleman's library so elaborate they are said to duplicate those from which the resourceful Scarlett O'Hara fashioned her green velvet gown in the movie *Gone with the Wind*. Information on Nottoway Plantation is available by telephoning 225-545-2730 or writing P.O. Box 160, White Castle, LA 70788. Nottoway Plantation is located on the Mississippi River on Hwy. 405, just off LA Highway 1 south of Plaquemine.

One Old Hunter's Receipt for Cooking Bear Claw

1 bear claw

Dig a hole in the ground and make it red-hot with live wood coals. Put the paw in this, properly dressed, and keep it there several hours, cooking it slowly but surely under more live wood coals until done to a turn. It is good, with a capital G.

Chef John Percle, formerly of Nottoway's Randolph Hall Restaurant, says if anyone brings him a bear claw, he will cook it (best not to invite the game wardens).

Nottoway's Mint Julep

4 oz. bourbon
2 oz. rum
2 oz. mint simple syrup
Fresh mint, orange slice, and a cherry for
    garnish

Stir together liquids and pour into a 12-oz. zombie glass filled with crushed ice. Garnish with fresh mint, an orange slice, and a cherry.

Mint Simple Syrup

8 oz. sugar
8 oz. hot water
½ tsp. pure mint extract (McCormack)

Combine sugar and hot water in Pyrex measuring cup and add mint extract. Stir well and allow to reach room temperature. Be sure all sugar is dissolved before using. Chill unused syrup. Makes 16 oz.

Soul in Yo Bowl

Who knew that cooking could be so sultry, so seductive, so downright sexy? But that was before listening to Chef Johnny Percle on his *Soul in Yo Bowl* CD, turning recipes into pure poetry in his deep, dreamy voice. And not since The Big Chill's *Heard It Through the Grapevine"* soundtrack have there been so many aroused souls dancing with abandon around a cookstove, at least not until Chef Percle rhythmically recited his recipes to the funky beat of his Cajun Lightfoot Band, jazzing up his jambalaya with Hank Williams' "Jambalay, Crawfish Pie, File Gumbo," stirring up a spicy gumbo with "ersters and swimps" on top of some down-home blues and zydeco.

Along the way this chef with the spoon in his hand and the song in his heart shares his lifelong love affair with Louisiana, hinting at the history of the state and its unique culinary and musical heritage, providing a travelogue from the Big Easy on up through plantation country and Baton Rouge politics, driving down Highway 1 "diggin' on the bayou and kissin' the setting sun." All to the accompaniment of childhood friend John Bergeron and some very talented back-up musicians, and all while rapping so passionately about the preparation of certain indigenous foods that the salivating listener can practically smell the spices simmering in the black iron pot and the andouille sizzling in the skillet. Mmn, mmn, what a delicious place to live!

In the *laissez les bons temps roulez* lifestyle of south Louisiana, a culture Percle celebrates with great passion, food and music have always been inseparably intertwined. But who would have thought to combine music and recipes to turn a mundane cookbook into a festive fais-do-do except Johnny Percle, DJ-rapper-bluesman-poet. He calls his CD dreaming out loud and shares on the soundtrack his philosophy of living: "Great Food,

Great Music and Great Friends = Majik!" Food fuels the soul, as he sees it, the soul delivers the music, and the chef's role is to put some of that soul in your bowl.

For Percle, combining these great creative influences into a single CD is a natural, given his background, which includes his own radio show as well as backstage catering to music legends from the Rolling Stones to Bob Dylan, before taking over Nottoway Plantation's elegant Randolph Hall restaurant.

Like many south Louisiana boys, Johnny Percle learned his cooking skills early, fixing sauce piquantes and gumbos at his father's hunting camp by the tender age of 10. For years he had watched his *maman* as she prepared the huge quantities of jambalaya and chicken stew dispensed through the country store his grandparents operated.

An apprenticeship with former army cook Boo Boudreaux, General MacArthur's personal chef, taught him how to cook in volume, which served him well when he went to work offshore. When the rig cook became ill, Johnny Percle said he could take over the job and do it better, and he did. His large portions and tasty dishes proved immensely popular with the roughnecks and launched him on a new career. Later working for Exxon in Alaska, his ingenuity came to the rescue when the oil workers turned up their noses at all the salad fixings supplied for their meals; the workers did like soup, though, and thus was born "Johnny Jam's Signature Bacon, Lettuce, and Creole Tomato Soup!"

By the age of 16, Percle began cooking for musicians in large arenas, and before long he was catering special events, performances, and big musical extravaganzas. It was New Orleans' own Dr. John who tagged him with the nickname "Johnny Jambalaya." Over the years he has cooked for and entertained the famous and the infamous, including Professor Longhair, the Neville Brothers, the Grateful Dead, Glen Campbell, Tanya Tucker, Diana Ross, Marvin Gaye, and even the fabulous Rolling Stones in 1981, when 90,000 fans filled the Superdome at the largest indoor concert ever held. When basketball great Shaquille O'Neal heard his CD, he started calling Johnny Percle the "Elvis of the Bayou."

Other than presiding over the dining room at Nottoway's elegant Randolph Hall since the 1990s, Chef Percle still travels the globe arranging and catering special events. With a huge amount of help and support from his immensely talented wife, Terry Thomassie-Percle, who has served as Nottoway's food and beverage director, he brings Louisiana's famous Cajun cuisine to such faraway spots as Rome, London, South America, Hawaii, Puerto Rico, and the Virgin Islands. He has cooked for big-time politicians and Pope John Paul II and has gone all the way to Alaska to put on special culinary events for the Iditarod dogsled races. He once cooked gumbo for 4,000 in Canada, and in one single day he fed such disparate diners as Chief Justice Warren Burger and the wild rock band Kiss.

Now, after having provided some of the best food in Louisiana at Nottoway on a daily basis (and this included dinner each evening), he's getting into the mass production of some of his special creations for marketing in stores and restaurants. Don't miss the bottles of his fantastic JJ's Herb Dressing & Marinade in Nottoway's gift shop.

Chef Johnny "Jambalaya" Percle likes honest and unpretentious Louisiana dishes, "soul in yo bowl" as he calls them, and into that bowl he crams a taste of culture, the entire history and heritage of the Bayou State, its music and poetry, landscapes and people, whom, he says, are like no other anywhere in the world. He considers it the highest praise when a reviewer calls his food "real," and that's just what it is. He shares a few of his favorite recipes here. The vegetable jambalaya was developed for Louisiana Public Broadcasting's series on heart-healthy cuisine.

Johnny Jam's Signature Bacon, Lettuce, and Creole Tomato Soup

1 lb. bacon, cut into 1" pieces
½ lb. butter
6 large tomatoes, cut into wedges
2 tbsp. Pickapeppa Sauce
2 tbsp. Lea & Perrin's Worcestershire Sauce
2 tbsp. Tony's Seasoning
1 10.5-oz. can cream of asparagus soup
1 qt. Half & Half
1 head of lettuce, cut into 1" pieces

Cook bacon in large saucepan. Remove bacon before crisp and set aside. Add butter to bacon drippings and tomato wedges. Add Pickapeppa, Worcestershire sauce, and Tony's Seasoning. Combine asparagus soup with Half & Half and heat thoroughly, but do not allow to boil. Add bacon back to soup. Serve over lettuce. Serves 6.
Recipe from Chef Johnny Percle.

Chef Johnny Jam's Fresh Mardi Gras Vegetable Jambalaya

2 cups turkey stock
1 clove garlic
⅓ tsp. fresh basil, chopped
⅓ tbsp. fresh thyme, chopped
⅓ tbsp. fresh oregano, chopped
1 tbsp. Creole seasoning
1 tbsp. picante sauce
1 green bell pepper
1 red bell pepper
1 yellow bell pepper
1 large red onion
1 bunch celery
1 yellow squash
1 zucchini
12 pea pods
12 carrot sticks
2 cups cooked rice

Bring stock to a boil in a large stock pot. Add garlic, basil, thyme, oregano, Creole seasoning, and picante sauce. Cut peppers, onion, and celery into one-inch pieces. Slice yellow squash and zucchini and cut slices in half. Lower the heat and slowly add all vegetables to flavored stock, being sure to distribute them evenly. Simmer 5 minutes to heat thoroughly. Add the cooked rice and blend well. Cover and simmer 3-5 minutes until liquid evaporates. Serves 8-10.
Recipe from Chef Johnny Percle.

JJ's Meaux Jeaux Pork Medallions

6 boneless pork chops (about 1½ lb. total)
¼ cup JJ's Herb Dressing & Marinade

Sauce
Juice of 1 lemon
Juice of 1 lime
⅓ cup orange juice
½ cup chicken broth
4 tbsp. salsa
4 tbsp. sweet orange marmalade
2 tbsp. JJ's Herb Dressing & Marinade
1 tbsp. Worcestershire sauce
1 tbsp. dark brown sugar

2 tbsp. olive oil
2 tbsp. JJ's Herb Dressing & Marinade
1 cup onion, sliced
2 tbsp. dry sherry
1 tbsp. minced garlic
½ cup chopped gold bell pepper
1 tsp. dried parsley
1 tsp. lemon pepper
2 tsp. cornstarch, dissolved in ¼ cup water
¼ cup sliced green onions

Rinse pork and place in shallow glass pan. Coat with JJ's Herb Dressing & Marinade (available from Nottoway Plantation). Chill 30 minutes while preparing remaining ingredients.

Combine sauce ingredients in a small glass bowl; set aside.

Place a non-stick skillet over medium-high heat until hot. Add 2 tbsp. olive oil and 2 tbsp. JJ's Herb Dressing & Marinade, swirling to coat bottom of pan. Add pork chops and brown for 2 minutes on each side; remove from pan. Add onion and reduce heat to medium. Sauté until onions are brown on edges. Add sherry and swirl to deglaze pan. Sauté 1-2 minutes. Add garlic, bell pepper, parsley, and lemon pepper to pan and stir well. Sauté 3 minutes over medium heat. Return pork chops to pan; reduce heat to low. Pour sauce over the chops, cover, and simmer 20 minutes, turning chops once. Uncover skillet and stir in cornstarch solution and green onions. Simmer uncovered 5-6 minutes, turning chops once. Serving suggestion: Place pork medallions on platter of Mardi Gras Jambalaya and top with sauce; garnish with orange slices. Serves 6.
Recipe from Chef Johnny Percle.

Bread Pudding

¼ lb. margarine, melted
1 cup water, warmed
1 loaf sliced white bread, broken in pieces
1 cup evaporated milk
½ tsp. vanilla
3 eggs, beaten
1 cup sugar

Mix in large bowl the water and margarine. Put broken bread into mixture and stir. Add milk and stir. Add vanilla, eggs, and sugar and stir well. Pour into a 12x16" baking pan and bake at 350 degrees for 1 hour. Serve warm, topped with rum sauce. Serves 20.
Recipe from Chef Johnny Percle.

Rum Sauce for Bread Pudding

1 stick butter
1 cup sugar
2 16-oz. whipped topping
6 oz. rum

Melt butter. Add sugar and mix together in a bowl until sugar is dissolved. Add whipped topping and whip mixture with a wire whip. Drizzle the rum into the mixture a little at a time. Cover and keep mixture in the freezer until ready for use. Serves 20.
Recipe from Chef Johnny Percle.

Madonna Chapel

Practically in the shadow of the South's largest plantation home, Nottoway, is a delightful, diminutive structure called "the world's smallest church," Madonna Chapel. Located on River Road (Highway 405) at Bayou Goula, just south of Plaquemine and north of White Castle, this tiny place of worship was built in 1903 by a poor Italian sugarcane farmer named Anthony Gullo.

When his eldest son fell desperately ill, Tony Gullo fervently prayed for his recovery and promised to erect a chapel dedicated to the Madonna if the child lived. The boy survived, and his grateful father built the finest chapel he could afford, a hectagonal chapel measuring only 7 feet along its sides, its tiny steeple topped with a simple cross. In this tight-knit community of Italian immigrants long known as Little Italy, rich in heritage but not material possessions, friends pitched in with small donations of lumber and funding to help Gullo fulfill his promise.

The centerpiece of the chapel was a fine statue of the Madonna ordered directly from Italy. Mass was celebrated regularly, and many of the parishioners walked along then-gravel River Road and picked flowers along the way for the altar. The chapel was so small that only the priest and 2 altar boys could fit inside; the congregants gathered beneath the towering pine trees just outside.

In the early days, the chapel was supported by raffles, with parishioners donating whatever they could spare to raise funds. The present-day caretaker recalls church members arriving for the raffles laden with homemade crocheted afghans or swinging live chickens by their feet.

When a new levee was constructed in 1924, the chapel had to be moved and reconstructed on a 9-foot-square plan, only slightly larger than the original. It faces the levee just across River Road and is always ready to welcome worshipers, as the key is kept in a marked box just to the right of the arched double entrance doors. In 2003, the Madonna Chapel celebrated its centennial with mass presided over by Bishop Robert Muench for more than 300 people, including some of the descendants of Tony Gullo, who came all the way from Illinois.

Farther down Bayou Lafourche, situated just beside LA 1 between Leeville and Golden Meadow, sits Smith's Memorial Shrine, another tiny wood frame chapel, this one on concrete piers backing up to the bayou. The double entrance doors are flung wide to welcome worshipers who might want

to stop awhile, light a candle, say a prayer, remember a lost loved one, and sign the guest register along with others from around the world. The entire structure measures about 10 by 14 feet and contains 4 tiny 2-person pews and an altar, with the stations of the cross decorating the walls. Beside the entrance repose 2 marble crosses, one inscribed "Livingston Smith 2-12-44 to 10-3-47, aged three" and the other "Abraham J. Smith, Jr. 7-22-49 to 6-14-66, aged sixteen."

Today, up the river at the Madonna Chapel, mass is celebrated every year on the Catholic Feast of the Assumption of the Blessed Mother, August 15, and the chapel anchors a community maintaining distinctly Italian cultural and culinary traditions in the midst of a sea of Cajun and Creole neighbors. On March 19 the hard-working cooks and bakers of the community offer St. Joseph altars, beautifully decorated stages laden with every food imaginable except meat: Italian cookies, fruits and breads, cakes and vegetables, fish and spaghetti, all of which are shared with the public and then donated to the poor. The altars are presented in thanksgiving or for favors asked through the intercession of St. Joseph, and they are a meaningful continuation of the Italian heritage of the community.

Mrs. A. J. Roppolo, who with her husband has served as caretaker for the Madonna Chapel since 1989, provides some of the traditional Italian recipes that usually make an appearance on the St. Joseph altars. Anyone wishing to make a donation to the upkeep of the chapel can do so through Mrs. Roppolo at 28160 Hwy. 405, Plaquemine, LA 70764.

Italian Fig Cookies

3 pkg. dried figs
3 15-oz. boxes raisins
1¼ cups pecans
1 cup fig preserves
Peeling and juice of 1 orange
2 cups Karo syrup
1½ tbsp. cinnamon
1½ tbsp. allspice
2½ lb. flour
7 tsp. baking powder
½ tsp. salt
½ lb. Crisco
1⅓ cups sugar
4 eggs
¾ cup milk
2 tsp. vanilla

Grind first 5 ingredients. Combine with corn syrup and spices and mix well to create fig filling. Set aside. Mix dry ingredients (except sugar) in large bowl. Cream Crisco and sugar together. Add eggs one at a time, beating after each addition. Mix vanilla and milk. Add flour mixture, milk mixture, and creamed mixture alternately, beating well after each addition. Use more milk if dough is too dry. Roll out cookie dough on floured board. Cut a strip about 3 inches wide. Using a cookie press, press filling of figs into center of strip. Roll edges together lengthwise and press to seal. Make slits along rolls at half-inch intervals. Slice into pieces 1½ inches long. Bake on lightly greased cookie sheet at 350 degrees until cookies are light brown.

Chocolate Ball Cookies

3 cups Crisco
2 cups sugar
2 eggs
1 tsp. vanilla
½ cup evaporated milk
7 cups flour
½ cup cocoa
2 tsp. cloves
7 tsp. baking powder

Glaze

1 cup confectioner's sugar
2 tbsp. milk

Cream Crisco and sugar until light and fluffy. Beat in eggs then add vanilla and milk. Combine dry ingredients. Add to creamed mixture and mix well. Roll dough into small balls, about 1 tsp. of dough each. Place on ungreased cookie sheet in a preheated 350-degree oven. Bake 15-20 minutes until done. For glaze, mix confectioner's sugar and 2 tbsp. milk thoroughly. Glaze cookies.

Pineapple-Cherry Italian Cookies

17 cups flour
2 cups sugar
16 tsp. baking powder
2 cups Crisco
4 cups pecans, chopped
1 cup cherries, chopped and drained
2 cups crushed pineapple, drained
3 eggs
1 qt. milk

Mix dry ingredients. Work in Crisco. Mix in pecans, cherries, and pineapple. Add eggs and milk. Roll dough into small balls. Bake at 350 degrees until lightly browned. Makes 20 dozen cookies.

River Road African American Museum

It's a small museum with a huge goal, that of collecting, preserving, and interpreting art, artifacts, and buildings related to the history and culture of African Americans in the little grassroots rural communities along the Mississippi River from Baton Rouge south to New Orleans. The museum is dedicated to telling the oft-neglected part of history in this stretch of the South, where a big percentage of the country's wealth was concentrated among the antebellum cotton and sugarcane plantations. Its thoroughly modern Web site flashes with a telling old African proverb: "Until the lion writes his own story, the tale of the hunt will always glorify the hunter."

Museum director and public historian Kathe Hambrick conceived the long-overdue idea of an exhibition recognizing the contributions of enslaved Africans on the Mississippi River plantations; thus the River Road African American Museum was founded in 1994. Its current location is on Charles Street in historic downtown Donaldsonville, but it already has plans to expand.

Future goals include restoration and reopening of 3 significant structures shedding additional light on early black experiences along the river: the local Rosenwald school, constructed in the '30s as the cornerstone for black public education, the 2-story True Friends Benevolent Society hall, begun as a mutual aid society when newly freed African Americans needed health and burial insurance, and the Africa Plantation House, which was first the home of Donaldsonville's earliest black doctor and later of the black inventor of an innovative sugarcane planting machine.

Present museum exhibits highlight free people of color, the river parish roots of many notable jazz musicians, rural black doctors and inventors, folk artists, the history of black education, the underground railroad, and the reconstruction period of rebuilding after the Civil War, when blacks played a pivotal role in local governmental affairs. The museum also serves as an international resource for genealogical research, maintaining extensive slave inventories from south Louisiana plantations as well as archives of documents, books, rare photographs, collections of artifacts, newspaper ads for runaway slaves, obituaries, and midwives' records.

In addition to these compelling exhibits, the museum sponsors guided tours and special events throughout the year, like the Juneteenth Freedom Festival of family gatherings, picnics, exhibits, arts and crafts, African dance, and music. The River Road African American Museum is open

Wednesday through Saturday 10-5, Sunday 1-5, and may be reached by telephone at 225-474-5553, by mail at 406 Charles St., Donaldsonville, LA 70346, or by email at aamuseum@bellsouth.net. The Web site is www.africanamericanmuseum.org.

Among its most interesting exhibits is the plantation kitchen, complete with curtains and aprons handsewn from old sacks that historically held chicken feed, rice, or sugar. Here visitors learn about the influence of African cuisine, culinary techniques, and foodstuffs like okra and yams on south Louisiana cooking. The African background of the black plantation cook undeniably added soul and spice to the plantation dining table, and indeed, Creole and Cajun cooking blends African, French, and Spanish influences, resulting in the spicy gumbo called Louisiana cuisine.

Okra, that tall member of the mallow family and related to cotton, probably originated around Ethiopia prior to the 12th century B.C. and was brought by slaves from West Africa to the Caribbean and United States in the 1700s. Also known as gombo, or gumbo, the name comes from one of the Niger-Congo group of languages, and in Louisiana, the Creole cooks quickly learned from slaves the secret to using the unique flavor and sticky texture of its long seed pods to thicken the soups that came to take its name. Growing up to 6 feet tall and thriving in Louisiana's brutal summer heat, okra can be fried, pickled, or sautéed with tomatoes and other fresh vegetables, but its enduring popularity revolves around that famous okra gumbo.

Fried Okra

Okra
Milk
Cornmeal
Oil
Salt to taste
Pepper to taste

Slice okra into ½-inch pieces and soak in milk. Drain well, dredge in cornmeal, and deep-fry until golden brown. Season well.

Seafood Okra Gumbo

1 lb. okra, sliced
4 tbsp. shortening
2 tbsp. flour
1 onion, chopped
1 bunch green onions, chopped
2 cloves garlic, minced
1 bell pepper, chopped
½ cup celery, chopped
2 tbsp. parsley, chopped
1 lb. can tomatoes
3 tbsp. tomato sauce
1 bay leaf
1 sprig thyme
1½ qt. water
1 lb. raw shrimp, peeled
½ lb. crabmeat
Tabasco to taste
Salt to taste
Pepper to taste

Fry okra in 2 tbsp. shortening until it ceases to rope. In large, heavy pot, make brown roux with remaining shortening and flour. Add chopped vegetables and cook until soft. Add fried okra, tomatoes, and seasonings. Simmer 45 minutes. Add shrimp and crabmeat, and simmer additional 30 minutes. Season to taste with salt and pepper. Serve over rice. Serves 6.
Recipe from Lucie Butler.

Chef John Folse

No one but Louisiana's beloved Chef John Folse, whose interests and enthusiasms encompass all the centuries and all the countries of the globe, would have the nerve, the absolute audacity, to even think of publishing an 850-page cookbook. Too big, said the naysayers. Too heavy. Too long. Too *fabulous,* said the buyers, who immediately snapped up several large printings of *The Encyclopedia of Cajun and Creole Cuisine* and clamored for more.

This should have surprised no one, for John Folse's secret to success has always been making magic from meager beginnings. It's the story of his life and the basis for his culinary philosophy: build upon your natural heritage, use fresh, native ingredients, and learn to appreciate simplicity. In other words, stay true to your roots and your region and to your heart and soul.

He was born on Cabanocey Plantation in St. James Parish, in the heart of sugarcane country but not exactly into the lap of luxury. His mother, Therese, died in childbirth in 1955, leaving his father with 6 sons and 2 daughters between the ages of 10 and 3. His father, Royley Folse, never remarried. Any woman, he was fond of explaining, who would marry a man with 8 children would have to be crazy, and the last thing a man with 8 children needed was a crazy wife.

A wonderful housekeeper named Mary Ferchaud was hired, and for 30 years she instilled in the Folse children, especially the boys, a love of good food and good cooking, working wonders with vegetables just picked from the family's one-acre garden, fresh seafood, wild game, and pork and poultry raised on the grounds of the plantation.

From these humble beginnings was born the Chef John Folse and Company, starting with a small restaurant, moving to a larger one, and then, with typical John Folse exuberance, taking "a taste

of Louisiana" worldwide and introducing the state's indigenous cuisine to such foreign locales as Japan, Beijing, Hong Kong, Paris, even Moscow during the presidential summit between Ronald Reagan and Mikhail Gorbachev. How to top preparing feasts for presidents? Chef Folse became the first non-Italian chef to create a Vatican state dinner for the pope in Rome.

Along the way he garnered tons of honors and awards and was officially named by the Louisiana State legislature as "Louisiana's Culinary

Ambassador to the World." But his recognition was not merely local or even regional. Congenial John Folse was named the American Culinary Federation's National Chef of the Year, and he also served as president of the prestigious nationwide American Culinary Federation, the largest organization of professional chefs in America.

His popular restaurant spawned other culinary endeavors: a catering and events management division at White Oak Plantation in Baton Rouge, a publishing company to produce his 7 marvelous cookbooks as well as works by other authors, an extremely popular international public television series, a radio cooking talk show (*Stirrin' It Up*, the best-tasting show on talk radio!) and nightly TV segment, and a giant, $4 million manufacturing company with its own USDA plant to custom-make more than 100 products for food-service distributors, retailers, and chain restaurants across the country. At Nicholls State University in Thibodaux, the Chef John Folse Culinary Institute opened in 1994, dedicated to preserving the state's rich cultural and culinary heritage while training the next generation of young chefs.

When fire destroyed his Lafitte's Landing restaurant in the old Viala Plantation house at the foot of the Sunshine Bridge over the Mississippi River in 1998, John Folse reopened the restaurant in the Bittersweet Plantation house where he and his wife had been living in Donaldsonville, then turned it into a bed and breakfast. A new pastry division called Exceptional Endings, which supplies baked goods to gourmet coffee houses, was soon supplemented by the Bittersweet Plantation Dairy, whose award-winning artisan cheeses, Bulgarian-style yogurt, and ice creams are sure to have a positive impact on Louisiana's flagging dairy industry. And then came a digital recording studio, described as a natural outgrowth of the radio and television projects.

Did we mention that John Folse's interests are broad? Along with that inborn Cajun ingenuity and gift of gab, he's amazingly adept at product development, production, and marketing. He fittingly refers to his megacompany as a corporate gumbo, and only Chef John Folse could manage to blend its disparate elements so satisfactorily and so successfully.

But of all his outstanding accomplishments in the culinary field, perhaps John Folse's most meaningful contribution has been to provide the definitive answer, once and for all, to the prickly question that since Louisiana's very earliest beginnings has been troubling cooks and diners, fueling arguments, causing fisticuffs, and if not actual shootouts then at least cookoffs: what the heck is the difference between Cajun and Creole cooking?

Folse finds the answer in the very romance and adventure of Louisiana's history and heritage, from the Native Americans who taught the earliest settlers the secrets of wild game and grains to the Italian immigrants, from the African influences of plantation slave cooks to the hearty Germans with their love of sausage making, from the classic cuisine of the French aristocrats to the Acadian deportees who learned out of necessity to make a tasty meal from next to nothing. Taking into account all those diverse influences, Chef Folse defines the resulting cooking methods in this way: Cajun is the French country cuisine that established itself in the bayous and swamplands of Louisiana around 1785, well-seasoned, one-pot meals using native raw ingredients, often with a dark roux base and plenty of onions, celery, bell pepper, garlic, green onions, and parsley to enhance the flavor of the coons and wild ducks, the alligators and turtles, the crabs and shrimp and fish and oysters, the deer and everything else they could catch or trap or shoot to put food in the hungry bellies of their large families. Creole cooking, on the other hand, Chef Folse calls an aristocratic melting-pot, many-coursed cuisine developed in New Orleans. It is the intermarriage of the 7 nations—Native American, French, Spanish, English, African, German, and Italian—that settled the city beginning in the late 1600s. And Louisiana cuisine, as Chef Folse defines it today, is the resulting happy union of the ingredients, flavors, and techniques of both Cajun and Creole.

As the early Creoles were themselves the children of the intermarriages of European aristocrats of several cultural heritages, so Folse traces the influences of these early founding cultures that united in Creole cooking: the Provence soup called bouillabaisse that formed the basis for gumbo, the spicy Spanish seafood paella that gave rise to jambalaya, the German charcuterie that became the boucherie for preserving pork in boudin and andouille sausage, the Italian taste for pastries and ice cream, the sauce piquantes and tomato base from the West Indies' and Haiti's exotic cookpots, the local produce and wildlife introduced by the native Indians, the okra brought from Africa by slaves that made gumbo what it is today. Says Chef Folse, "Creole cuisine is that melange of artistry and talent, developed and made possible by the nations and cultures who settled in and around New Orleans."

Cajun cooking, by contrast, mirrors the history and survival skills required of the French exiles cast out from Acadia in Nova Scotia in 1755, *le Grand Dérangement* memorialized in Longfellow's epic poem, *Evangeline*. The 10,000 Acadians were driven from their homes, their village of Grand Pre burned, and their families separated and dispersed on 24 British vessels that dumped them at various ports in North and South America and even Europe. Some were reunited in south Louisiana, where waves of the desperate refugees struggled to make a new home, living off the land in the swamps and marshes and cooking native foodstuffs without the exotic spices and classic ingredients available to the Creoles in New Orleans. Creole cuisine boasted a rich array of many courses with close ties to European aristocracy, but in a single black iron pot the resourceful Cajun cooks could combine local products, wild game, seafood, native vegetation, and herbs into tasty jambalayas, grillades, étouffées, stews, fricassees, gumbos, and sauce piquantes. Says Chef Folse of Cajun cuisine, it is a "table in the wilderness, a creative adaptation of indigenous Louisiana foods. It is a cuisine forged out of a land that opened its arms to a weary traveler, the Acadian."

A few of Chef John Folse's recipes are reprinted here; more are available from his Web site at www.jfolse.com, where his cookbooks and other products can also be purchased (telephone 225-644-6000).

Fried Green Tomatoes

1½ cups oil
3 green tomatoes
1 cup flour
Salt
Black pepper
1 tbsp. basil, chopped
1 cup seasoned Italian breadcrumbs
1 cup milk
1 egg
1 cup water
Louisiana Gold Pepper Sauce

In a 10-inch cast-iron skillet, heat oil to 350 degrees. Slice tomatoes ½ inch thick and drain on a paper towel. Season flour with salt and pepper. Add chopped basil to the breadcrumbs. Prepare egg wash by combining milk, egg, and water. Blend well using a wire whisk. Season to taste using salt, pepper, and Louisiana Gold. Dredge tomato slices first in flour, then in egg wash, and finally in breadcrumbs. Pan-fry a few at a time until golden brown on each side. Remove and drain well. Eat as a salad topped with a remoulade or tartar sauce. Serves 6.
Recipe from Chef John Folse.

Creole Cream-Cheese Pecan Poundcake

¼ cup pecans, chopped
3 cups cake flour
½ tsp. salt
¼ tsp. baking soda
1 cup unsalted butter
3 cups white sugar
6 eggs
1 tsp. vanilla extract
1 cup Bittersweet Plantation Dairy Creole
    Cream Cheese
⅓ cup all-purpose flour
½ cup packed brown sugar
1 tsp. ground cinnamon
2 tbsp. melted butter

Preheat oven to 300 degrees. Grease and flour a 10-inch bundt or tube pan. Sprinkle pecans on the bottom of the pan and set aside. Sift together flour, salt, and baking soda in a medium bowl and set aside. In a large bowl, cream butter and white sugar until light and fluffy. Beat in eggs one at a time, and then stir in the vanilla. To this add flour mixture alternately with Creole cream cheese. Pour half of the batter over pecans in prepared pan. In a small mixing bowl, add ⅓ cup flour, brown sugar, and cinnamon, and mix well. Cut in butter until mixture resembles coarse meal. Sprinkle mixture over batter in the bundt pan and add remaining batter over cinnamon-sugar mixture. Bake 75-90 minutes or until a toothpick inserted into the center of the cake comes out clean. Let cool in pan for 20 minutes, then turn onto a wire rack and cool completely. Serves 12.
Recipe from Chef John Folse.

Praline Bread Pudding Cake

5 10" loaves French bread
1 qt. milk
6 whole eggs
1½ cups sugar
1 oz. praline liquor
¼ cup vanilla
1 tbsp. cinnamon
1 tbsp. nutmeg
1 tbsp. vegetable oil
1 cup chopped pecans
1 cup raisins

Slice French bread into ½-inch round croutons. In a large mixing bowl, combine milk, eggs, and sugar. Using a wire whisk, blend ingredients well. Add praline liquor, vanilla, cinnamon, and nutmeg. Continue to blend until all ingredients are well mixed. Oil a 10-inch cheesecake pan. Press 1 layer of French bread croutons into the bottom of the pan, making sure there are no void spaces. Sprinkle a small amount of pecans and raisins over this layer. Ladle in ⅓ of the custard mixture. Carefully press the custard into the croutons using the tips of your fingers. Continue this process until croutons have been covered and all custard is used. You may find that ½ cup of the custard mixture will remain once the pan has been filled. This is normal and you must continue to add the custard a little at a time, firmly pressing into the croutons until all has been used. This may take an hour or so. Always allow the bread pudding to set in the refrigerator overnight before cooking. When ready to bake, preheat oven to 375 degrees. Place the bread pudding pan into a larger pan partially filled with water. Cook in this water bath approximately 1-1½ hours. Serve warm or cold. Slice into 14 wedges to serve 14.
Recipe given to Chef John Folse by master bread pudding chef Sharon Jesowshek.

Alligator Chili

3 lb. alligator meat, diced
½ cup oil
2 cups diced onions
1 cup diced celery
1 cup diced bell pepper
2 tbsp. diced garlic
2 tbsp. diced jalapeños
1 16-oz. can pinto beans
3 8-oz. cans tomato sauce
1 cup chicken stock
1 tbsp. chili powder
1 tsp. cumin
Salt to taste
Cracked black pepper to taste

In a heavy Dutch oven, heat oil over medium-high heat. Add alligator and sauté 20 minutes to render juices. Add onions, celery, bell pepper, garlic, and jalapeños. Sauté until vegetables are wilted, approximately 3-5 minutes. Add pinto beans, tomato sauce, and chicken stock, then bring to a low boil and reduce to simmer. Add chili powder and cumin, stir well into mixture, and allow to cook one hour, stirring occasionally. Once alligator is tender, season to taste using salt and black pepper. This dish is always served at hunting camp dinners over spaghetti. Serves 6.
Recipe from Chef John Folse

Oak Alley Plantation

Ah, the trees. Oak Alley's 800-foot-long allée of 28 spectacular live oaks, their huge limbs straining skyward to form a vaulted canopy over the approach to the house, is certainly the most magnificent in Louisiana, and just as surely one of the most magnificent in the world. The trees, 300 years old and some more than 30 feet around, were planted in the early 1700s by an unknown hand, no doubt an early French settler, leading to some small, long-gone dwelling. The oaks were spaced 80 feet apart, allowing them room to reach their full, majestic development. Predating the present house by at least a century, the live oaks connect it with its Mississippi River landing and make approaching the house akin to entering the aisle of some stupendous, towering cathedral, shady and silent and awe-inspiring.

Nearly as impressive are the 28 immense free-standing Doric columns that have encircled the home since it was built in the late 1830s for Jacques Telesphore Roman, member of an illustrious French Creole family (a brother was governor and a sister was wife to prominent planter Valcour Aime, who sold Roman the Oak Alley property in 1835). Jacques Telesphore Roman, in 1834, took as his wife the beauteous young French Quarter belle Marie Therese Celina Josephine Pilie, and for her he built a mansion in the quiet sugarcane country that he hoped would be magnificent enough to take her mind off the gaiety of the New Orleans social scene. Alas, it worked only partially.

The Greek Revival house, some 70 feet square with 2 stories and an attic topped with a belvedere, was originally named Bon Sejour, good rest, but

the famous live oaks, clearly visible from passing steamboats on the Mississippi, won it a nickname that soon supplanted the real one. Brick kilns on the place turned out the huge quantities of brick used for flooring and pillars as well as the 16-inch-thick walls to keep out the heat. Cypress trees of immense girth were ringed and aged and then cut in the swamps for the rest of the construction. The lower gallery was floored in brick, flush with the ground; the upper gallery had a wood railing with a sheaf design carved by hand. The house was said to have been designed by Celina's father, and sensibly, too; deep verandahs shade the interior while doors, windows, and transoms on each side of the house face each other to encourage the cross ventilation needed to alleviate Louisiana's oppressive summertime heat. Over the 16-foot mahogany dining table, the punkah stirred the air just enough to cool the diners without snuffing out the candles.

To the rear of the house were rows of slave cabins, 28 in all, housing 93 field hands and 20 house servants, including a cook trained in the culinary schools of Europe. An inventory of J. T. Roman's estate, dated April 1848, the year he died at age 48, listed all 113 slaves, including children, with name, age, value, and skills as well as racial classification (African Negro/Negress, American Negro/Negress, Creole Negro/Negress, or Mulatto).

The house would provide a fitting backdrop for a fine Creole family. The Creoles were native-born children of European, often aristocratic parentage, who initially viewed the rustic and uncouth Americans moving into their river region with contempt. From the French Quarter of New Orleans, where French was the spoken language and civilized Old World ways prevailed, the Creoles carried their refinements and extravagances into the countryside as they developed sugarcane plantations extending upriver.

The wonderful Louisiana writer Harnett Kane, a devoted student of plantation life, in the 1940s wrote of an encounter between Valcour Aime and a distinguished French traveler who, in the way of French travelers, was rather overly impressed with himself. After the 2 gentlemen found common ground discussing the subtleties of wines, the delicacy of sauces, and the richness of desserts, the overbearing Frenchman made the mistake of commiserating with Aime regarding the sad deprivations that must surely be experienced by a man of such good taste and discrimination in the uncivilized wilds of Louisiana. A wager was placed, and

the Frenchman was invited to dine upon a typical Creole meal at Valcour Aime's Mississippi River plantation.

The crab and shrimp gumbo, with its green okra and special spices, was served over rice, followed by a fricassee of terrapin, then breast of wild duck, snipe, quail, mushrooms, platters of greens flavored with salt meat, a luscious dessert combining the tartness of wild cherries with liqueur and tantalizing tropical fruit, cheeses, coffee, cigars, 4 or 5 wines, and a most pleasant brandy. The Frenchman savored every course, then attempted to collect his winnings, vowing that the ingredients for such a fine meal could not possibly have been grown on the plantation.

Valcour Aime led his guest to the turtle pens in the marsh behind the house, opened the hothouse door to reveal tropical fruits growing, and showed the tobacco patch from whence came the makings for the cigars, the vineyard where grapes were grown for the wines, the moist places sprouting mushrooms galore, and a greenhouse from which were harvested the coffee beans. The overbearing Frenchman could not help but admit defeat.

Within the last century Oak Alley was beautifully restored by Mr. and Mrs. Andrew Stewart, who had

the foresight and good sense to establish a non-profit foundation assuring the continuing preservation and upkeep of both house and grounds, which are meticulously maintained. Tours today open the door for guests to experience the cultured lifestyle of the early Creole planters of the River Road.

Hoop-skirted guides well versed in antebellum lore give daily tours in the soft French inflections of south Louisiana, explaining how in the parlor only the gentlemen enjoyed the heady rum made from sugarcane, while the more delicate ladies had to make do with pears, but those pears were liberally laced with the very same rum. They demonstrate how the coiled courting candle signaled the time for a propitious departure by suitors; how the low dining room chairs were well suited to accommodate men whose average height was 5' 4" and ladies considerably shorter; how the headboards of the rolling-pin beds had detachable rollers for smoothing and fluffing moss mattresses. They describe how one extra bedroom was designated for guests or the sick or as a viewing room for the deceased. Many of the children of the family died young, succumbing to the dreaded plague of yellow fever or tuberculosis, and in the nursery a nanny

sat up all night to watch over them, guides explain. The sugar kettles scattered across the grounds and the immense wooden skimmer in the plantation office pay tribute to the property's early raison d'etre, and to this day it is still surrounded by broad, flat fields of green growing sugarcane waving in the breeze.

Besides house tours and a bed and breakfast in the outbuildings, Oak Alley provides a spectacular setting for weddings and receptions, corporate meetings, and all manner of large gatherings. Popular special events include the spring Arts and Crafts Festival, which brings more than 150 vendors of arts, crafts, and food to the grounds, and an annual Christmas Bonfire Party that's the perfect celebration of a Creole Christmas, including the traditional bonfire burning on the levee.

Oak Alley Plantation is on the Mississippi River on LA Highway 18 near Vacherie. The Oak Alley Restaurant and the Plantation Café/Ice Cream Parlor provide a wonderful selection of dining opportunities for visitors for both breakfast and lunch, and many favorite recipes from the restaurant and from the family are included in *Oak Alley Plantation Cooking,* a hard-cover book of 225 pages with spectacular color photographs, available in the plantation gift shop or online from www.oakalleyplantation.com or by telephone from 800-442-5539.

Chicken and Sausage Gumbo

½ cup oil
½ cup all-purpose flour
1 cup onion, diced
½ cup celery, diced
½ cup bell pepper, diced
1 tbsp. Italian seasoning
1 tbsp. parsley flakes
½ lb. andouille, sliced
1½ lb. boneless chicken breast
½ lb. smoked sausage, sliced
4 cups water
2 tbsp. Tony Chachere's Creole Seasoning
1 tbsp. sugar
¼ cup piquant sauce
1 bay leaf
2 cups chicken broth

Heat oil in heavy 8-qt. pot. Add flour, stirring constantly until roux is the color of a copper penny. Lower flame. Add onion, celery, bell pepper, Italian seasoning, parsley flakes, andouille, chicken, and sausage. Add 2 cups water, cover pot, and sauté on low for 30 minutes, stirring every 5 minutes to prevent sticking. Add remaining ingredients and cook for one hour, stirring every 15 minutes or so to prevent sticking. Skim off grease and remove bay leaf before serving. Serve over steamed white rice. Serves 10.
Recipe from Oak Alley Restaurant.

Gateau Sirop (Syrup Cake)

1 cup peanut oil
1 cup brown sugar
1 cup cane syrup
⅓ cup molasses
4 eggs
2 tbsp. vanilla
1 cup boiling water
2 tsp. baking soda
2 cups sifted all-purpose flour
2 tsp. ground ginger
2 tsp. ground cloves
2 tsp. ground cinnamon
¾ cup chopped pecans (optional)

Preheat oven to 350 degrees. Beat oil, brown sugar, syrup, molasses, eggs, and vanilla in mixing bowl. Combine boiling water with baking soda and add to syrup mixture. In a separate bowl, combine flour, ginger, cloves, and cinnamon. Gradually add liquid a little at a time to flour mixture until well mixed. Bake in greased cupcake pans, filled ⅔ full, for 15 minutes. Remove from oven and sprinkle with chopped pecans. Return to oven and bake until a toothpick inserted in the center comes out clean (approximately 5 minutes). Makes 24 muffins.
Recipe from Oak Alley Foundation.

Shrimp Althea

3 lb. raw shrimp, peeled and cleaned
¼ cup onion, minced
5 tbsp. butter
8 oz. mushroom, sliced
¼ tsp. liquid shrimp and crab boil
1 tbsp. salt
Pepper to taste
2 tbsp. flour
1½ cups sour cream

Sauté shrimp and onion in 4 tbsp. butter until shrimp are pink. Add mushroom slices and remaining butter. Sprinkle in crab boil, salt, pepper, and flour, and cook for 1 minute. Add sour cream and cook, carefully stirring until smooth. Serve with steamed rice or noodles. Serves 8.
A Chef John Folse recipe for Oak Alley Restaurant.

Crawfish-Stuffed Potatoes

6 medium baking potatoes
4 tbsp. butter
½ cup onion, chopped
1 clove garlic, minced
1 lb. crawfish tails
1 tsp. evaporated milk
1 tsp. salt
½ tsp. black pepper
½ tsp. cayenne pepper
2 cups cheddar cheese, shredded
½ tsp. paprika

Preheat oven to 425 degrees. Scrub potatoes well and dry thoroughly. Place in oven and bake until they can be pierced with a fork, about 45 minutes. Melt butter in skillet. Add onion, garlic, and crawfish tails. Simmer until done. Cut potatoes in half lengthwise. Remove center and whip with electric mixer. Add crawfish mixture, milk, salt, black pepper, cayenne, and 1 cup of cheese. Fill potato shells. Sprinkle with remaining cheese and paprika. Return to oven and bake at 425 degrees for 15 minutes. Serves 6.
Recipe from Oak Alley Restaurant.

Spuddy's Cajun Foods

On Highway 20 in Vacherie, Spuddy's Cajun Foods is a little restaurant that isn't fancy or expensive. But look at all the pickup trucks in the parking lot at lunchtime, and you know this is where to go for good old down-home Cajun cooking.

Spuddy, whose real name is Maitland—but he'll be embarrassed if you tell anybody—was always interested in cooking and learned from observing his mama and grandparents and watching the guys at the hunting camp. But he went off to college and worked as a computer programmer. It was not until he went into sales and had to visit many of the small restaurants and food markets in the area that he realized what he really wanted to do. What Spuddy Faucheux really wanted to do was own his own business, and he really wanted that business to involve food. It was his passion.

In Vacherie he found Folse's Seafood and Meat Market. It wasn't a restaurant, it wasn't serving food, and it wasn't very large, but owner "Mr. Peanut" Folse had something Spuddy craved: a smokehouse. And so, in 1993, Spuddy purchased the market and launched a new career. He credits Mr. Peanut with sharing recipes and teaching him the

techniques of smoking andouille, sausage, turkey necks, and all the special ingredients that make his cooking the epitome of local Cajun cuisine.

Now Spuddy makes all his own sausage—fresh, smoked, venison, chicken, all kinds—and does all the food preparation except the plate lunches, which are made by 70-year-old Ruby Charles, accomplished cook and mother of 9. She started working with Spuddy when they just had one little stove and she believed him when he promised her that one day they'd have 2 stoves and be able to cook side by side. Spuddy also promised his wife, Elaine, that one day they would have a business where they would be able to work together, and she must remind herself what a blessing she thought that would be, now that they arrive at the restaurant at 5:30 every morning and are still there late into the evening. Spuddy loves it so much that even on his rare days off, he spends all his time cooking and creating new recipes.

As for the smokehouse, the 4x4-foot block building that could hold 60 pounds of andouille or 90 pounds of smoked turkey necks, well, Spuddy did just great learning how to smoke the meats. However, he must have missed a little something in the safety lessons because one day, thanks to a volatile mixture of propane gas and hot coals, he blew the whole building up and nearly killed himself in the process. But, as Spuddy says, one thing leads to another, and at the next restaurant association trade show he found a bigger smoker, and this one could be used to barbecue as well, so besides now smoking 300 pounds of andouille or 360 pounds of turkey necks at one time, barbecued ribs, briskets, pork, and chicken are additional specialties of Spuddy's Cajun Foods. Despite the large size of the smoker, Spuddy says he fills it up several times a week, and since it's on wheels, he can cater offsite as well.

Chef Spuddy Faucheux's house specialties include chicken-andouille or seafood gumbo, crawfish stew, red beans and rice, jambalaya, white beans, and rice dressing. Seafood specialties include stuffed crabs as well as shrimp, oysters, and

fish in platters, po' boys, and boats. And there's plenty of fried chicken, andouille po' boys, even appetizers of fried okra or onion rings. When he says his hamburgers are homemade, he means it, since he grinds the chuck right in the kitchen to make the patties, and when he says his seafood is fresh, he means he's just picked it up from the docks down at Bayou DuLarge or Dulac, just bought the crawfish out of the Atchafalaya Swamp, or just trapped the crabs himself. No imported seafood here, whenever possible, promises Spuddy, who has seen low-priced imported seafood driving local fishermen and shrimpers out of business, selling their boats, and going to work in the oilfield.

Spuddy likes to think of his restaurant as having an old-time country store atmosphere, a friendly, unhurried place to relax and enjoy good food and good conversation. It's famous among the tour guides as "where the locals eat," which is the gospel truth, and it's just what tourists are looking for. In the winter, the locals know it as a "one-stop gumbo shop," where they can get everything they

need to make a big pot of gumbo, from chopped seasonings and okra to fresh crabs, oysters, andouille, and smoked sausage or chicken, gizzards, whatever they want to include. The local workforce loves the prepared foods waiting in the cooler, usually the leftovers from the plate lunch specials the day before, so that they can take jambalaya, white beans, rice dressing, or red beans for their lunch break at work.

The food is attraction enough, but don't miss the décor. Spuddy's wife, Elaine, whose mama was a Gravois from "back Brusly" who didn't learn English until she went to school, has collected dozens of vintage photographs showing area scenes and plantations from the 19th century and early years of the 20th century. She started with a few photos from the local historical society, then found that customers were bringing in other historic pictures to share. Soon she had a veritable museum of life along River Road. The photographs are fascinating vignettes: the parish priest in black hat and long vestments feeding his chickens, a number of sugar plantation mansions before restoration and a few that later would be lost to flooding or deterioration, old country stores and car dealerships, and other nostalgic scenes. Allow plenty of time to peruse this invaluable collection scattered across the walls of the restaurant.

Like all good Cajun cooks, Spuddy Faucheux doesn't really use written recipes and never actually measures one single thing, but his wife, Elaine, has done her best to pin him down on specifics so he can share some of his favorites here.

Roux

1 cup oil
1 cup flour
2 medium onions, chopped
2 small or 1 large bell pepper, chopped
½ stalk celery, chopped

It is best to make roux in a black cast-iron pot for consistent distribution of heat. Heat oil. When oil is very hot, slowly add flour, using whip or spoon to stir. Continue stirring until roux is the color of caramel. Roux should be consistency of paste. If roux is too thick, add a little oil and continue stirring. When satisfied with the color and consistency, add onions, bell pepper, and celery. Cook on low fire 10-15 minutes. This will stop the roux from cooking further and darkening. Put roux aside to add to dishes to thicken and flavor them.
Recipe from Spuddy Faucheux.

Okra and Seafood Gumbo

½ cup oil
2-4 lb. okra, chopped
2 medium onions, chopped
½ stalk celery, chopped
2 small bell peppers, chopped
2 gal. water
Roux
1 lb. andouille
1 tsp. liquid crab boil
4 lb. shrimp, peeled
2 lb. white crabmeat
2 lb. lump crabmeat
Salt and pepper to taste

Heat oil in pot. Add okra, onions, celery, and bell peppers. Smother until okra is no longer crunchy. Stir constantly. While okra is cooking, boil water. Slowly add roux to boiling water until gumbo is consistency of thick soup. Add andouille and boil on medium fire for 20 minutes. Add okra to water along with crab boil. Boil on medium fire for 10 minutes. Add shrimp and crabmeat. Slow boil for 5-10 minutes. Season with salt and pepper to taste. Serve over rice. Serves 8-10.
Recipe from Spuddy Faucheux.

No-Roux Gumbo

½ cup oil
4 lb. cut okra
2 small onions, chopped
1 bell peppers, chopped
½ stalk celery, chopped
2 gal. water
2 lb. andouille
2 lb. smoked sausage
Smoked turkey necks, optional
5 lb. chicken leg quarters
2 tbsp. parsley flakes
Season-All
Cayenne pepper

Heat oil in saucepot. Add okra, onions, bell peppers, and celery. Let smother until soft and slime is cooked out of okra. Stir constantly. While okra is cooking, in stock pot bring water to boil, add andouille, sausage, turkey necks, and leg quarters. Boil meat until tender. Remove meat and debone as necessary. When okra is smothered, add to boiling stock and slow boil for 15 minutes. Add sausage, andouille, and poultry. Slow boil for 15 minutes. Add parsley flakes, season to taste, and serve over rice. Serves 8-10.
Recipe from Spuddy Faucheux.

Smothered Cabbage

1 large head of cabbage or 2 small heads
½ cup oil
1 lb. andouille, sliced, or meat of your choice
2 medium onions, chopped
Season-All to taste
Cayenne pepper to taste

Cut head of cabbage in half. Slice into large pieces or break apart. In stock pot, add oil and cabbage. Add andouille and chopped onions. Smother for about 30 minutes. Season to taste. This is any easy dish to prepare. Use your imagination, and add turkey necks, pig tails, pickled meat, ham or any of your favorite meats; smothered cabbage is always good. Serves 6.
Recipe from Spuddy Faucheux.

Crawfish Stew

½ cup oil
4 lb. crawfish tails
1 gal. water
Roux
1 tbsp. parsley flakes
Season-All
Cayenne pepper

In black iron pot, heat oil, add 3 lb. crawfish tails, and sauté 10-15 minutes on medium heat. Remove crawfish tails. Add gallon of water to pot. When water comes to a boil, add roux 1 tbsp. at a time, and stir until consistency of thick soup. Add other 1 lb. crawfish tails. Simmer on low fire for 30-45 minutes. Add parsley flakes and smothered tails, and cook for 15 minutes. Season to taste. Serve over rice. Serves 8-10.
Recipe from Spuddy Faucheux.

Laura: A Creole Sugar Plantation

This is a historic house tour that is so well presented in such a lively and unique fashion that visitors hardly even noticed when the entire house itself was temporarily off-limits due to damage from a disastrous fire. But then the tour here isn't about old furniture or fabrics, fascinating as they can be, the tour here is about the people who made this house a home, who lived and wrote its history, who still have the power to reach across the generations and make it come alive, house or no house. For Laura is more than a house tour; it is a Creole family album.

Uniquely situated in place, time, and history to tell the story of Louisiana's Creole population, Laura was built in 1805 just as the Creole culture in the state reached its zenith, in between the fading of the French colonial period and the Spanish regime and the arrival of the adventurous Americans who poured in after the Louisiana Purchase opened the rich lands of the Mississippi delta. On tour, visitors learn that during this period of history, south Louisiana's population was predominantly Creole—and Creole meant a blending not so much of blood as of the cultures so instrumental in writing the state's early history, the Europeans (mostly French and Spanish), the West Africans, the Native Americans.

Early Louisiana historian and writer Lyle Saxon, whose classic *Old Louisiana* was first published in 1920, noted that the Creoles, "for all their luxury, were essentially simple in their tastes. They liked good food and comfort. Their houses were strong and austere. Ornate elegance came into fashion only twenty years before the Civil War."

The Creoles would leave the showing off to the *arriviste* Americans they considered so gauche, and consequently Creole architecture for many years was underappreciated, as visitors marveled instead at the immense and impressive Greek Revival mansions built from the 1830s through the 1850s, during the height of prosperity in plantation country. Now, Laura, with its shocking bright red roof, ochre walls, and intense green trim, stands in stark contrast to its ubiquitous white-columned neighbors, at long last serving to increase awareness and appreciation of this earlier, simpler style dwelling.

Visitors today disembark from buses rather than steamboats, but once they leave the parking area to stroll through the thick, lush plantings of bananas and palms and other tropical vegetation onto the plantation grounds, they find themselves in the world of 19th-century Creole Louisiana. The 11 historic structures on the place, many of them in absolutely original and unrestored condition, vividly illustrate the tour guide's talk.

Much of the tour is based upon *Memories of the Old Plantation Home,* completed in 1936 by Laura Locoul Gore to open a window onto her Louisiana Creole past for her own children, so far removed from the sugarcane fields of her childhood. This is the Laura for whom the plantation was named when she was 13 years old. She died in 1963 at the

age of 101, and her manuscript was not discovered for another 30 years after her death. That manuscript helped turn Laura Plantation into one of the most remarkable stories of salvation in the 20th century.

The plantation's literary tradition exceeds the story of the family. Some African folktales about the rascally Compair Lapin, told by the early slaves on the plantation, were translated into English and published in 1894 by Laura's distinguished neighbor Alcée Fortier. These stories are considered some of the earliest recordings of the Br'er Rabbit tales later made famous by Joel Chandler Harris in his *Uncle Remus* stories, which were based on similar folktales circulated among West African slaves in his home state of Georgia.

For many years Laura languished lazily in a state of disrepair, until the Tulane School of Architecture nudged in its direction preservationists Norman and Sand Marmillion. For a decade Norm Marmillion, head of the River Parishes historical society and one whose roots in Louisiana go back to 1703, had already known of the folk tale connection to Laura, and he had grieved as one after another of the old river plantations declined and disappeared through neglect, flood, hurricanes, fire, and vandalism.

When Laura was sold at auction, the St. James

Sugar Co-Op LLC outbid the Marmillions, who only found out about the sale the day prior. The co-op still owns the place, but the Marmillions, not to be deterred, put together a group of investors in a business called the Laura Plantation Company and managed to lease the house and surrounding 13 acres on a long-term renewable basis, with Norm as president and principal of the company. And then the fun began, as the Marmillions turned into amazingly accomplished international sleuths and put heart and soul into searching out Laura Plantation's story.

For much of its most recent century, the Florian Waguespack family farmed the property. They had no early photographs, but they did have an old letter, dated 1967, from a Mrs. Charles Gore in St. Louis, mentioning how her mother-in-law had enjoyed revisiting the plantation. Attempts to make contact through the return addresses failed; most of the addressees were deceased.

Not to be deterred, the Marmillions called all 64 Gores in the St. Louis telephone book, finding on the 62nd call the grandson of Laura Locoul Gore, which led to a family friend's old address book in New Orleans, which led them back to St. Louis to one Clyde Norris. When they called Mr. Norris, his immediate response was that he had been waiting for 14 years for their call, for it was to him that Laura's memoirs has been entrusted with instructions to keep them until someone from Louisiana called for them. The memoirs put the Marmillions in touch with family connections in Paris, who offered access to related collections in the French Archives Nationales, as well as portraits and photographs of the plantation.

Laura Plantation had begun with one Monsieur Guillaume DuParc, banished from France after killing a young man in a duel, only to become a Revolutionary War hero and Spanish commandante in this country. He was rewarded with land grants that became the 12,000-acre Laura Plantation. Guillaume died in 1808 at age 52 "on the plantation, musket in hand, the owner of 27 pairs of white muslin pantaloons," leaving behind explicit instructions that his property should never be sold to an American in order to avoid "trickery and bad chicanery from this sort of people." The registry of slaves on his plantation, recorded upon his death, had listings of slaves both skilled and unskilled; apparently among the latter was "Patience, age 24, a black woman coming from Moco, and her son Tantale, age 18 mos.; she has no redeeming qualities at all."

The home DuParc constructed was raised high above the ground on brick piers, the upper floor in the *briquette-entre-poteaux* style and a cool

bricked wine cellar on the ground level. The plantation included a detached kitchen to the rear, barn, warehouses, and a small sugar mill. A lane stretched behind the house for 3½ miles, lined on both sides with slave quarters, 69 cabins in all. By the 1850s, the plantation was home to 100 mules and 195 humans, of which 175 were slaves. Within a decade the plantation's yearly harvest included 460,000 pounds of sugar, 30,000 gallons of molasses, 7,500 bushels of corn, and 100 bushels of sweet potatoes.

DuParc's daughter Elizabeth married Frenchman George Raymond Locoul, and their son Emile was the father of Laura Locoul Gore, who was born in 1861, the year the Civil War began. In her 101 years of life, she saw many changes in the culture and society around her, lived through both the flush times and the hard times of plantation life, and learned enough to know that her own personal fulfillment would be found elsewhere. She had watched her grandmother and mother harden under their burdens in this all-consuming Creole family business and seen firsthand the shocking abuses of slavery, like the brand burned into the face of a captured runaway slave, old Pa Philippe.

Laura announced her engagement to a gentleman from St. Louis, far removed from the Louisiana sugarcane country. In the newspaper appeared an announcement that on Saturday, March 14, 1891, would be sold at auction "the Laura Sugar Plantation in the Parish of St. James" on "long credit and low interest," 725 arpents more or less, a good sugar-house, 26 mules, and a full supply of agricultural implements, 2 dwelling houses and stables, "famous for its productiveness and the situation is considered one of the most desirable in the sugar producing section." But not until the Marmillions came along did the Laura Plantation recover enough to resume its rightful place in the march of history. Now the plantation, located on LA 18 at Vacherie (telephone 888-799-7690; online www.lauraplantation.com), is open daily for tours in both English and French, tours made all the more enjoyable by their very uniqueness and candor.

For the children of the plantation in the early days, life sometimes moved too slowly, and in between the horseback rides and the music lessons, Laura confesses to sitting on the upper gallery watching the steamboats pass by on the Mississippi River and wishing 2 of them would collide to provide some excitement. It was in 1876 that young Laura had her first taste of freedom, when she was allowed to go to school in New Orleans, first as a boarder and then as a day student living with her

grandmother on Toulouse Street behind the French Opera House. Her great joy was attending performances with a cousin and watching during the intermission when the gentlemen would go out to purchase *pattes toutes chaudes* and bring them back for the ladies to eat, ever so delicately, in their white gloves, as well as pastry shells filled with oysters or chopped meat.

Laura's old nurse, Anna, walked her to and from school with a group of friends. On the way home, they would often stop and buy coconut cakes and pralines from the street vendors, and Laura recalls in her memoirs how "in New Orleans old negro women went around with baskets on their heads, calling out, *'Callas, toute chaudes,'* 'piping hot Callas,' which were rice cakes shaped in a shell. They also carried *'vol-au-vents,'* those light, meat and sauce-filled pastries that some of us called 'fly-aways,' or *'volaille,'* which was cooked chicken."

Callas

1 cup uncooked rice
2 cups water
3 medium eggs
3½ tbsp. sugar
2¼ cups flour
1½ tsp. baking powder
1½ tsp. nutmeg
2 tsp. ground cinnamon
½ tsp. salt
Vegetable oil

Cook rice by bringing water to a boil, stirring in rice, reducing heat, and simmering until all water is absorbed, approximately 15-20 minutes. When rice is done, set aside to cool. Beat eggs and sugar with an electric beater for approximately 2 minutes. Add rice to this mixture and stir together until rice is well coated. Sift together all dry ingredients. Slowly add the dry ingredients to the coated rice, stirring well. Divide rice dough into 8-10 equal portions and round into 2"-diameter balls. In a deep fryer, heat oil, approximately 3-4 inches deep, to a temperature of 350 degrees. Deep-fry several rice balls at a time until golden brown and crusty. Dry on paper towels. Callas are best sprinkled with powdered sugar but can also be eaten with anything sweet like jelly or cane syrup. Makes 8-10.

Pralines

1½ cups white sugar
1 cup dark brown sugar
½ cup evaporated milk
½ tsp. salt
½ stick oleo
2 cups pecans, broken into pieces
2 tbsp. vanilla

Mix white sugar, brown sugar, milk, and salt in stir-fry pan. Bring to a rolling boil. Boil 2 minutes; agitate but do not stir. Add oleo and stir until oleo is melted. Remove from fire. Add pecans and vanilla and beat until thick and creamy. Drop by spoonfuls onto wax paper. Make one batch at a time, but do not try to make these in rainy weather. Makes 14 pralines.
Recipe from Margaret Shaffer.

Little Shrimp Pies

1 cup mixed seasoning vegetables (chopped celery, onion, bell pepper)
⅓ cup butter
2 cloves garlic, minced
1 lb. shrimp, peeled and chopped
Tony Chachere's Cajun Seasoning to taste
2 tbsp. parsley, minced
2 tbsp. green onions, chopped
½ cup Cheddar/Swiss cheese mixture, grated
2 cups biscuit mix
⅔ cup water
Oil

Sauté seasoning vegetables in butter until soft. Add garlic, shrimp, and Tony's seasoning, and simmer 10 minutes. Add parsley and green onions. Stir in cheese after mixture cools, and then make crust. To make crust, combine biscuit mix with water. Stir dough with fork, knead, and roll out on floured board. Cut into 4-inch circles. Place spoonful of cooled filling in center of each circle, fold in half, and seal end with fork. Deep-fry in oil until browned. Serves 6-8.

St. Joseph Plantation

When it was decided to share the home and history of St. Joseph Plantation with the public, the family members came together to help ready the 1830 house to meet the public. All of the family members. All 205 of them! They were all members of the St. Joseph Planting and Manufacturing Company, Ltd., a family corporation dedicated to collectively raising sugarcane on 2,500 acres of family land comprising the old St. Joseph and Felicity Plantations and restoring the old family house. Most recently they have diversified into a barge lease on the river and ownership of a profitable sandpit as well.

St. Joseph Plantation is on the Mississippi River just south of Oak Alley, near the little community of Vacherie. Vacherie, roughly translated, means cow pasture, and before sugarcane became the staple crop, the area was settled by German immigrants who had large cattle operations. This is, after all, the Cote des Allemands, the German Coast, and the first German cattle farmers arrived in the area in the early 1700s. Sugarcane preceded them, coming in the 1600s from the West Indies,

but it was not until Etienne de Boré perfected the granulation process that sugar became known as white gold and the cattle pastures along the Mississippi River were transformed into immense, flat fields of sugarcane, the tall stalks waving in the breeze in orderly rows as far as the eye could see.

It was in 1877 that Joseph Waguespack moved here from St. Charles Parish, having originally come to this country from Alsace-Lorraine, and it is his descendants who have banded together to put their money and hard work into the restoration of the home their ancestors purchased at a sheriff's sale just after the Civil War, paying $25,000 for 1,000 acres.

So this is a family operation; family members still raise sugarcane on the rich alluvial topsoil of the property, family members still live on the place, and family members give a warm welcome to visitors coming to hear family recollections. As for the house and the surrounding dependencies, it's a restoration in progress, which makes it all the more interesting.

St. Joseph Plantation's main house is a raised

Creole structure, the main living quarters perched high on brick piers to escape the spring floodwaters and catch the cooling breezes off the river. The lower floor has walls of brick 14 inches thick; the upper floors were done in the construction method called *briquette-entre-poteaux*, brick between posts. In the bathing room the walls are left uncovered so that visitors can view this building method—slave-made river clay bricks laid between handhewn cypress beams—unobstructed.

One early resident was the acclaimed American architect H. H. Richardson, and another, who purchased St. Joseph from the Scioneaux family who built it, was the early French doctor, one of Napoleon's royal surgeons, Dr. Cazamine Mericq, who made the rounds of the plantations in his horse-drawn buggy, caring for the residents of the big houses and of the slave quarters as well. The home doubled in size when it was occupied by the daughter of prominent planter Valcour Aime along with her husband and 10 children, but for the most part it remains in the original condition, allowing visitors to marvel at the early architectural sensi-

tivity to such vital necessities as cross ventilation, "nature's air conditioning," facilitated by 90-foot-long galleries shaded by awnings, 13-foot ceilings, and dozens of carefully positioned French doors and windows that made life bearable in the hot, humid Southern summers.

St. Joseph was one of the last of the Creole plantation houses to be built, and in fact it shows a few intrusions of the Anglo attachment to Greek Revival that became all the rage as the 1830s plantation prosperity opened the door for increasing American settlement along the river. The Greek key design of the large doorway from the upper front gallery into the central hallway shows this transitional influence and makes the house of particular interest to architectural historians.

But on tour, no matter how interesting the architectural detail, this house becomes a home, peopled with a fascinating array of residents who come alive as family members tell stories they heard as children. Joseph Waguespack had 8 children. His 2nd daughter, the Widow Trosclair, had 2 daughters who married 2 Simon brothers, and

each couple had 11 children; they all lived together in the St. Joseph house, raising 22 children together. Articles of clothing are on display that have been worn by children in the family, one after another, for more than a century.

The mourning room, dedicated to furthering an understanding of Creole mourning customs, has French *imortelles,* which were used to decorate graves on special holidays, and mirrors veiled in black netting in respect for the dead. Here visitors hear the sad stories of the male relative who broke his spine falling from a ladder while doing house repairs, the female relative burning leaves in the backyard wearing a long skirt that caught fire when the wind shifted, and the incredible saga of the father who, when a cyclone struck while he was enjoying the parish fair with his 4 children, rushed them into the shelter of the church and threw himself atop their small bodies to protect them from the winds, only to be struck in the head by a hatchet wielded by a rescuer trying to remove fallen beams. The children survived; the father did not.

There are photographs of the last full-time residents of the house, the widow and children who survived the cyclone, and 2 old maiden aunties,

Tante Blanche and Tante Olympe. Both loved to cook. Creole families always had soup or gumbo as a first dinner course. Tante Blanche's specialty was a hearty vegetable-beef soup, and a steady stream of relatives arrived each Sunday with containers to fill full of that dish. Tante Olympe was the baker in the family, and her angel food cake was considered the fluffiest around, though no one can quite remember whether it was supposed to contain 15 or 30 eggs. Her recipe for "Maspin," probably something akin to marzipan, has been preserved, in her handwriting, and in French. Other family favorites included Floating Island for holiday desserts, its tiny red spots of currant jelly topping dollops of meringue adrift in a sea of custard. At Christmas, so many cookies were baked that they filled more than a few 50-pound lard cans. The old aunts also made wine, and one family member still uses their recipes to make some just for the family: cherry bounce and wine made of pears, plums, kumquats, satsumas, blackberries, or strawberries.

St. Joseph Plantation, open for tours daily, is located at 3535 Highway 18, Vacherie, LA 70090; telephone 225-265-4078; online access www.stjosephplantation.com, or email stjoe@charterinternetcom.

Vegetable-Beef Soup

4 lb. beef and soup bone
4 qt. cold water
1 can tomatoes
2 onions, sliced
1 Irish potato, chopped
1 sweet potato, chopped
2 carrots, diced
1 sprig parsley, chopped
4 pieces celery, chopped
2 bay leaves
10 black peppercorns, whole
12 tsp. salt
Dash cayenne pepper
1 tbsp. butter
1 tbsp. flour
2 eggs, hard boiled and chopped
2 lemons, sliced
1 cup wine

Boil meat and bone in water for 2 hours, then add ingredients through cayenne pepper. Boil 1 additional hour. Remove vegetables (may be discarded or added to soup at end) and add to soup 1 tbsp. butter rubbed with 1 tbsp. flour, eggs, sliced lemons, and wine. Cut meat into small pieces, return to soup, and serve hot. Serves 8-10.

Angel Food Cake

⅛ tsp. salt
Whites of 12 eggs
1½ tsp. cream of tartar
1½ cups sifted sugar
1 cup sifted flour
1 tsp. vanilla

Add salt to whites of eggs and beat until frothy, then add cream of tartar and beat until stiff enough to stand up in peaks. Very slowly fold in sifted sugar, then fold in flour, taking 7 minutes each to complete these steps. Add vanilla. Bake in an ungreased angel food cake pan for 45 minutes at 350 degrees for the first 30 minutes, then increasing heat to 375 degrees during the last 15 minutes. Cool in inverted pan. Serves 8.

Mandarin Liqueur

6-7 mandarins, peels only
1 qt. good brandy or grain alcohol
Sugar
Water

Infuse peels in alcohol for one month. Filter and sweeten as desired with simple syrup in same quantities as alcohol made by boiling sugar and water together.

Floating Island

1 qt. milk
3 eggs
½ cup sugar
½ tsp. salt
1 scant tbsp. cornstarch
2 tsp. sugar
Vanilla
Currant jelly

Heat milk. Separate eggs. Mix sugar, salt, and cornstarch, then add to slightly beaten yolks. Beat egg whites until very stiff, add 2 tsp. sugar, and beat lightly. Spread egg whites on top of hot milk and cook on stove over medium heat for 3 minutes. Lift out with a skimmer and set aside on a plate. Pour hot milk on beaten yolks. Put this mixture into a double boiler and stirring constantly, cook until it thickens to consistency of cream. Don't overcook or it will curdle. Cool, add vanilla to flavor, and pour into serving bowl. Put cooked whites, in dabs, over top, placing specks of currant jelly on the whites. Serve cold. Serves 8.

Madewood Plantation

Magnificent Madewood rises from the cane fields like a classical Greek temple. That was only fitting, of course, for the family seat of the sugar dynasty's royalty, the Pugh family. In the mid-19th century, there were so many Pughs planting sugarcane along Bayou Lafourche that the standing joke was: Why is Bayou Lafourche like the aisle of a church? And the answer, naturally: Because there are Pughs (pronounced pews) on each side.

The Pughs moved to Louisiana in the early 1800s from North Carolina, but they traced their family heritage back to Owen Glendower, prince of Wales. Louisiana writer Harnett Kane, noting that Glendower boasted in Shakespeare's pages that "the earth did shake when he was born," quoted a later generation of Pughs agreeing that there was nothing unusual in the sentiment, for the Pughs had always thought well of themselves.

Initially there were three Pugh brothers who settled along Bayou Lafourche, planting first cotton and then sugarcane on expanding acreage of rich lands. They were among the first Anglo-Americans in the area, among the first to use slave labor to work their ever-widening fields, which soon engulfed the small farms of their French Acadian neighbors, and among the first to have steamboats traverse the bayou to transport their huge shipments of barrels of molasses and hogsheads of sugar, back in the days when Bayou Lafourche was at least 5 times wider at the Madewood landing than now. The brothers—Dr. Whitmell, Augustin the oldest, and Thomas the youngest—each had his own properties (more than 20 in all), and each built a family home. Upon reaching marriageable age, these wealthy Episcopalians amidst their poor Catholic neighbors

found suitable brides only among the few other Anglo families along the bayou. Some Pugh suitors in ensuing generations, according to Harnett Kane, seeking the nearest thing to perfection, even wooed and wed other Pughs.

But of all the accomplishments of the Pugh family, the most enduring is surely Col. Thomas Pugh's Madewood, 8 years in the planning and the building, substantial and made to last. Cypress timbers handhewn or "made" on the place (hence the name) were seasoned for 4 years before construction began in the mid-1840s; 60,000 bricks were baked by slaves on the property. When the house was completed, the interior walls were 18 inches thick, outer walls 24 inches thick, and the brick foundations extended 8 feet below ground. It is considered one of the finest examples of pure Greek Revival architecture in Louisiana and in the South.

Designed by famed New Orleans architect Henry Howard, Madewood reflects the upper South origin of the Pughs, setting it apart from most other Louisiana plantation houses of the time. It is much closer in design to mainstream America's interpretation of classical Greek Revival than most neighboring big houses and has been said to resemble more closely a great institution like a world bank, fine library, or classic courthouse than a family home. A beautifully proportioned peaked pediment replaces the usual low-pitched hipped roof of other Louisiana manors, and the heavy, elaborately carved Ionic pillars soar upward from a stylobate on the front gallery rather than small brick piers.

Henry Howard was an engineer as well as an architect and master builder, and he utilized all his background skills in fitting the house out for comfort in the hot, humid climate, situating it on one of the highest sites along Bayou Lafourche (22 feet above sea level) and facing the bayou to catch the cooling breezes off the waters, with floor-to-ceiling guillotine windows, high ceilings and extended galleries, spacious rooms, and plastered finishes over the thick, insulating brick walls.

There are 2 flanking wings echoing the design of the central core of the structure. Ceilings range from 15 to 24 feet in height, set off by interior columns and magnificent decorative moldings of plaster mixed with horsehair. Huge sliding pocket doors with original etched-glass panels and faux bois finishes separate the men's and ladies' parlors, and floors are of heart pine. With more than 20 rooms,

Madewood made a fine house for a fine, large family with 15 children, but Col. Thomas Pugh did not live to see its completion. After he succumbed to yellow fever in 1852, his formidable widow, Eliza, finished the house, added a 48-foot-long ballroom in one of the wings, saved the plantation from destruction during the Civil War by appealing to the Union general's Masonic ties with her late husband, hired her former slaves as sharecroppers, and generally kept the place intact and even profitable.

Today, the house is a National Historic Landmark filled with the fascinating antiques and carefully collected artwork of Keith Marshall and his wife, Millie; Keith's parents, Harold and Naomi Marshall, purchased and restored the home in 1964. Never one to avoid a challenge, Mrs. Marshall had one of the earliest French Quarter art galleries in New Orleans and in 1929 was the first woman to swim across the Mississippi River there, a fearless approach to life that no doubt stood her in good stead as she confronted the daunting prospect of reclaiming Madewood, especially with a husband whose repeated plaint was, "But I don't want to live in the country." The renovation was a staggering undertaking, for Madewood had been unoccupied for several decades, its beautiful ballroom piled high with hay. During the Civil War, when Federal troops occupied nearby Napoleonville, stabling their horses in the Episcopal church and using the Tiffany windows for target practice, the grounds of Madewood were used as a hospital, but the house was spared the torching and total destruction that occurred elsewhere.

The fascinating original kitchen and carriage house, the old family cemetery, and other historic structures moved onto the property surround the house. Tours, which can be custom-tailored to the special interests of visitors, are given daily except on major holidays, and elegant overnight accommodations are available in the main house and an 1830s raised steamboat captain's cottage. Welcoming wine and cheese are available for overnight guests in the library, and candlelight dinners feature regional specialties in the elaborate dining room, followed by brandy or coffee in the parlor and full breakfast in the morning.

The *Los Angeles Times* calls Madewood "a masterpiece of understatement," with no phones or televisions. Madewood's own advertising speaks of a return to gracious living at "a Louisiana house party on the bayou." What is provided here amid the canopied 4-poster beds and the candlelight suppers is pure and simple Southern hospitality at its best.

Madewood Plantation may be contacted by telephone at 800-375-7151, by mail at 4250 Hwy. 308, Napoleonville, LA 70390, or online at www.madewood.com.

Artichoke-Stuffed Chicken Breast

6 well-drained artichoke hearts, cut in half
6 boneless chicken breasts
6 slices bacon (turkey bacon can be substituted)
2 tbsp. unsalted butter
2 tbsp. flour
1 cup white wine (optional)
3 cups scalded milk (4 cups if omitting wine)
½ medium onion, finely chopped
1 pt. mushrooms, sliced
Salt and pepper to taste

Place 2 artichoke halves on chicken breast and fold breast in half. Wrap one slice of bacon around chicken breast; hold in place with toothpick. Set chicken breast aside. In a saucepan, melt butter and flour, and whisk until light brown in color. Gradually stir in wine and scalded milk, then add onion and mushrooms. Add salt and pepper, and season to taste. While sauce cooks about 15 minutes, layer chicken breasts in oven-safe pan. Pour sauce over chicken breasts and bake covered at 350 degrees for 1-1½ hours. Serves 6.
Recipe from Madewood Plantation.

Pinault Mint Syrup

8 oz. mint leaf
1¾ cup water
14 oz. sugar

Combine all ingredients and boil for 10 minutes. Filter to remove leaves. Keep refrigerated until used; can be stored up to one month. Great to add to water for a refreshing mint taste or to make mint juleps.
Recipe from Madewood Plantation.

The Edward Douglass White House: Louisiana State Museum

Just north of Thibodaux on LA 1, there is a simple raised cottage of handhewn pegged cypress built in 1824. But it has been designated a National Historic Landmark for its associations with several generations of remarkable men, for this early farmhouse was home to Judge Edward Douglas White, 7th governor of Louisiana and a U.S. senator, and his son, Edward Douglass White, Jr. (who added an additional S to his middle name), also a U. S. senator and the only Louisianian to serve as chief justice of the U. S. Supreme Court, a body upon which he served for nearly 3 decades.

They were distinguished men, these Whites, but they came from a long line of men who, known for their eccentricities, were unusual, restless spirits rarely content to stay in one place for long. The senior E. D. White's father, Dr. James White, studied divinity, law, and medicine and was known in Tennessee for occasional drinking bouts during which he dressed in buckskins and invited strangers upon the streets to share his gourd of whiskey. One account, quoted in the well-researched book *Paths to Distinction,* written by William D. Reeves and published by The Friends of the Edward Douglass White Historic Site, says of Dr. White, "When he was in his sprees, his originality and humor made him the admiration of the vulgar; when sober, of the learned and talented."

Dr. White's courtship of the mother of his son Edward Douglass was just as offbeat, the same written account recording it as practically an abduction of a young girl called Sukey who'd caught his fancy, mounting her behind him on his horse as he dashed through North Carolina to a session of Congress, the girl dressed in boy's clothing to be passed off as his body servant. On the return trip,

says this account, the young lady became "unable to proceed and was delivered a son."

Dr. White died in 1809; his son Edward Douglas, 15 years old, left home the next year to attend what would become Vanderbilt University then returned to Louisiana to read law and commence a legal practice. When he was elected to Congress to represent a district extending from New Orleans along Bayou Lafourche, he began buying tracts of bayou land to establish a plantation, even though he would spend most of his time in Washington until his campaign for state governor began in the early 1830s.

It was on a campaign trip through the state that E. D. White and his party were aboard the steamboat *Lioness* on the Red River when the boat caught fire and exploded. Written accounts quoted in the Reeves book report that the whole boat was blown to smithereens except the ladies' cabin, whose floor was flung intact upon the water with several ladies afloat on it. When the smoke cleared White was seen swimming, terribly burned and temporarily blinded. Said the account, "The ladies were in their night-clothes; but what will not woman do to aid the distressed, especially in the

hour of peril? One of the most accomplished ladies of the State snatched from her person her robe de chambre, and throwing one end to the struggling Governor, called to him to reach for it, and with it pulled him to the wreck."

A remarkable road to distinction for a remarkable man, who recovered from his injuries, was elected governor in 1834, served his gubernatorial term, and then returned to Congress. When White died in 1847, his body was brought up to Thibodaux from New Orleans by steamboat in a floating funeral procession, with stops along the way for mourners to pay their respects.

The 18-arpent plantation White assembled along Bayou Lafourche in the 1820s and '30s had first been settled by the Acadian families of Pierre Arcement, who arrived from France in 1785 aboard the ship *La Villa D'Archangel,* and Jean Baptiste Trahan, who arrived the same year aboard the *St. Remi.* E. D. White combined 8 smaller properties to make up his plantation, following the land-use pattern of the period that saw small Acadian farms consolidated into larger sugar plantations when the value of sugar rose. Thus Lafourche landowners had

ready access to transportation for their sugar via the new Barataria and Lafourche Canal linking the bayou to New Orleans markets. When White's congressional term ended, the family lived on the plantation and implemented a number of improvements, including a new sugar house. Their son Edward Douglass White, the 4th of their 5 children, was born there in 1844.

The raised Acadian cottage the Whites occupied was sturdily built of wood siding over bousillage walls, with front and rear stairs to the main upper living floor and plenty of ventilation through French windows and doors. Soon after the death of Governor White, a number of home improvements were effected, and his widow spent considerable time shopping for furnishings and plantation supplies, often in New Orleans, where she also found a 2nd husband. Her shopping lists included such items as rice, tea, coffee, cracked sugar, cider vinegar, claret, spices, sperm candles, cheese, hams, starch, smoked beef, bottles of Madeira and Tenerife, barrels of potatoes, bottles of olives, soda biscuits, sides of bacon, cashmere shawls, black parasols, fiddle strings, lace curtains and panes of glass, saddle and bridle, mule shoes, straw bonnets,

calico and linen, oyster gridirons and other cooking and dining utensils, black walnut armoires and bedsteads and marble-topped washstands, clothing and toys for the children and other supplies like brogans and rough yardage for the 58 slaves, all delivered to her steamboat for shipment to the plantation, and all charged on credit to the commission merchants who sold the plantation sugar crop for her.

Only 2 when his father died, Edward Douglass White, Jr. was raised on the plantation, which for a time was one of the top sugar producers on the west bank of Bayou Lafourche. After his mother's remarriage, he also spent considerable time in New Orleans, attended Catholic schools, fought in the Civil War, graduated from Tulane Law School, and then launched his own remarkable legal and political career. In 1874 he was first elected to the state legislature. At age 35 he was appointed associate justice on the Louisiana Supreme Court and by 1894 was representing his state in the U.S. Senate. It was President Cleveland who appointed E. D. White to the U.S. Supreme Court and President Taft who appointed him as chief justice. Sitting on this highest bench he earned widespread recognition for his intellect and integrity, energy, courtly manners, and abiding love for justice.

Justice White had a consuming respect for the dignity and sanctity of the court. When, at age 49, he quietly married a widow originally from New Orleans, one of the presiding priests explained away the need for secrecy prior to the ceremony by saying, "Justice White felt a little delicate about appearing before the public in the role of a lover, I suppose, for you know the judiciary is almost like the clergy in dignity and reverence, and the idea of love-making in connection with a judge is as incongruous as it would be in the case of a bishop."

While he was otherwise occupied in the seats of power and justice, Justice White's plantation on Bayou Lafourche was occupied and operated by tenants. The last occupants of the house were the family of Leon Naquin, a large hardworking blacksmith and sugar boiler whose tiny wife, Mathilde, presented him with 11 children who slept in the attic. The French-speaking Naquins lived there from 1905 until around 1924 with no running water, no indoor plumbing, no electricity, and a large bread oven in the yard.

Now the home and 6 acres surrounding it are

owned by the state as a historic site and state museum; rather than a house museum furnished as a home, the site is utilized as an interpretive center and contains an interesting display examining the sugarcane industry, Bayou Lafourche culture, and of course the fascinating families who lived there. Special educational events are scheduled throughout the year to involve the community by bringing in real artisans to demonstrate early skills and practices like dueling ("the duel of honor was always the gentleman's recourse against slander and insult"), Civil War reenactments, and children's games of the 19th century. The autumn Bayou Lafourche Heritage Day draws hundreds to see artisans produce Chitimacha baskets, Acadian wooden toys, Creole split-oak baskets, ropes, and bousillage, while other experts demonstrate old-time spinning, weaving, wood carving, cistern making, boatbuilding, blacksmithing, and fine art.

In Washington, Justice White, a man of immense physical as well as intellectual stature, was said to set a rich table on par with that of the French ambassador. When he returned to New Orleans in 1894 during the court's summer recess,

a banquet was given in his honor, the menu reading as follows: Consommé Julienne and River Shrimp, Broiled Pompano with Sauce Reserve and Saratoga Chips, Sweetbreads on Toast with Champignon, New Potatoes and Cream Sauce, Spring Lamb and Mint Sauce, Mais Sans Branches, Salade Française, Fillet de Boeuf Demi Glace, Stuffed Tomatoes, Pommes Jardaire, Mais Gateau and Lubec Asparagus, Ice Cream, Strawberries, Assorted Cake, Fruits, Roquefort Cheese, Bent's Crackers, and Café Noir, foods typical of 19th-century upper-class repasts.

But on the plantation, the meals were considerably simpler, especially for the postbellum tenant families with their large numbers of mouths to feed. They ate plenty of indigenous foods, which were trapped in the wetlands, caught in the waters, and raised on the land, and they stretched the dishes as far as they could go with plenty of rice and beans, and rice and beans, and more rice and beans. But there were sweet treats as well, like Tarte à la Bouillie. For information on the Louisiana State Museum-Thibodaux (E. D. White Historic Site), telephone 985-447-0915.

Tarte à la Bouillie

Crust
½ cup butter
1 tbsp. Crisco
2 cups sugar
4 eggs
2 tsp. vanilla
1 tbsp. baking powder
1 tsp. baking soda
¼ tsp. nutmeg
Pinch of salt
4 cups flour
¼ cup milk

Cream butter, Crisco, and sugar. Add eggs and vanilla; stir. In a separate bowl mix together dry ingredients. Alternately add dry ingredients and milk to butter and sugar mixture, beginning and ending with dry ingredients. Roll dough ¼-inch thick on floured board. Using ⅔ of the rolled dough, line the bottom and sides of a 9-inch pan. Reserve ⅓ dough for top of tarte. Fill pan with vanilla custard.

Vanilla Custard
½ cup flour
⅔ cup sugar
¼ tsp. salt
4 cups milk
2 tbsp. vanilla
½ tsp. nutmeg (optional)
2 tbsp. butter

In a saucepan, combine flour, ⅓ cup sugar, and salt. Add enough milk to make a paste. Slowly stir in remaining milk. Place over medium heat. Cook, stirring constantly until mixture thickens and comes to a near boil. Cook 1-2 minutes. Remove from heat and mix in the remaining sugar. Return to heat. Bring mixture to a boil, stirring constantly. Remove from heat. Add vanilla, nutmeg, and butter. Stir approximately 5 minutes while cooling. Pour into prepared crust. Decorate top with ½-inch strips of remaining dough, making a lattice weave. Bake at 350 degrees for 45 minutes. Serves 8.
Recipe from Joyce Naquin's Maman Percle.

Couche-Couche

2 cups cornmeal
1 tsp. salt
1 egg
1 tsp. baking powder
1 cup hot milk
1 tbsp. oil

Mix cornmeal, salt, egg, and baking powder with hot milk. Mix well. Put oil in iron pot and add mix. Cook 30 minutes; stir. Serve in a bowl with fresh milk. This is an old Cajun breakfast dish. Recipe from Joyce Naquin's Maman Percle.

Tarte à la Bouie

4 cups heavy whipping cream
3 eggs
1¼ cups sugar
2 tbsp. cornstarch
2 tbsp. vanilla
¼ cup melted butter
Pinch of cinnamon
Pinch of nutmeg
2 9-inch pie shells, uncooked

Preheat oven to 350 degrees. In a heavy-bottom saucepan, heat cream until scalding. In a large mixing bowl, combine eggs, sugar, and cornstarch, and using a wire whisk, blend until creamy. Add vanilla, butter, cinnamon, and nutmeg, and continue to whip until all ingredients are well blended. Once cream has come to a low boil, ladle 1 cup into egg mixture, stirring constantly while pouring. Once well blended, pour egg mixture into hot cream and stir continuously. Remove from heat and allow to cool slightly. Pour slightly cooled mixture into one of the pie shells. Using a sharp paring knife, cut the other pie shell into ½-inch strips. Lattice the strips across the top of the pie in a decorative fashion. Place pie on center oven rack and bake for 45 minutes or until crust is golden brown.
Recipe from Chef John Folse.

Naquin's Bed & Breakfast

Frank and Joyce Naquin invite their guests to "come pass a good time," and they're not kidding. They extend Cajun hospitality at its very best, and to stay in their B&B in Thibodaux is to experience the unique culture of the area to the fullest.

Both from families of Acadian descent, the Naquins grew up in Thibodaux and never moved far from home. Joyce's driving tour for visitors is peppered with "This was my mama's house," "This is my cousin's house," "This is the house where I grew up," and "This is my sister's house." You get the picture; she knows the area and just about everybody in it. She remembers the old *mamans* and *grandmères* always cautioning the innocent young Thibodaux girls about those wild boys from Houma, just down the bayou. Those Houma boys, she recalls being warned, they don't stay close to their homes and their families like they should, and wouldn't you miss your mama? She heeded the warning and remains close to her extended family, many of whom still live in Thibodaux or the close-knit surrounding settlements like Choupic and Choctaw and Chackbay.

Joyce was born on Leighton Plantation after it became the Leighton Factory owned by Lafourche Sugars, where her father and other family members worked. In the late 1930s the factory revived a sugar mill deserted for more than a decade due to disease and low prices, then turned it into a productive operation grinding over 825,000 tons of cane in 1938, a year when there were nearly 50 other sugar mills in operation in the state.

Knowing the area as intimately as she does, Joyce makes sure her guests don't miss a thing in historic Thibodaux, which was settled around lands granted in 1801 by Baron de Carondelet to Henry Schuyler Thibodaux, who would later serve as Louisiana's governor. It was incorporated in 1838

during the governorship of another hometown hero, Judge Edward Douglas White, who also represented the area in the United States Senate. Located on Bayou Lafourche, the town was an important early trading center and shipping point for sugar, molasses, moss, and cotton; even mail was delivered along the waterway, with mail packets picking it up at the head of the bayou from riverboats from Natchez and New Orleans.

Spicing up her tour with an insider's knowledge not found in any tour book, Joyce points out all the major attractions, including the historic houses of worship. Considered the oldest Episcopal church west of the Mississippi River, St. John's Episcopal Church was begun in 1843 under the supervision of Bishop Leonidas Polk, its vestibule and slave gallery added a few years later. More than 40 live oaks over 150 years old shade the cemetery, where the earliest grave dates from 1838. Here Gov. Francis Nicholls rests in peace sans the left leg and arm lost in battle, and a nearby grassy knoll contains graves of Union and Confederate soldiers killed in the Battle of Lafourche Crossing.

Also in Thibodaux is the impressive Renaissance Romanesque St. Joseph Co-Cathedral, patterned after European cathedrals and towering over a busy boulevard, with elaborate ceiling frescoes painstakingly executed along its vaulted ceilings, magnificent stained glass windows relating Biblical stories, and a relic from the arm of St. Valerie. Considered Thibodaux's patron saint, St. Valerie was a virgin martyr beheaded in Rome during the Christian persecutions in the late 2nd century. The relic was obtained on a visit to Rome by the local priest in 1867, who wanted inspiration for *les jeunes filles* toward piety. It was sealed in an elaborately dressed waxen statue of a young girl and laid in a reliquary, shipped across the ocean, and then transported up from New Orleans via Bayou Lafourche in 1818 aboard the steamboat *Nina Simmes*. When it was placed on the altar of St. Joseph's, the ceremonies were attended by more than 4,000 people, and all businesses in Thibodaux were closed for the occasion. The young girls of the parish marched in the processionals wearing the white dresses of virginity with ribbons and wreaths of red, the color of martyrdom, the color of blood. In May 1916, St. Joseph's caught fire, the flames beginning in the sacristy, and when it became apparent that the church itself could not be saved, the cries went up: "Save St. Valerie! Save St. Valerie!" Local volunteer firemen and other citizens valiantly rescued the reliquary, and when the co-cathedral was rebuilt, St. Valerie was transported back aboard a fire truck in a solemn procession; every year during the Fireman's Fair a special firemen's mass is celebrated in thanksgiving for their heroism. The celebration features a parade that began in the 1850s.

But Joyce Naquin's tour includes a whole lot more than just the tourist highlights. "See that Walgreens over there?" she asks, pointing to a business constructed on the banks of Bayou Lafourche. "They have a drive-in window there, and their first customer was an alligator!" And then there's the simple stone cross on the banks of Bayou Lafourche, where the local faithful gather to pray to the Lily of Mohawks, the Blessed Kateri Tekakwitha, whose intercessions in the '30s healed one of the sisters of the Mt. Carmel Convent, which had been just across the street from where the cross stands today. After losing her family to smallpox that left her scarred and nearly blind at age 4, she converted to Catholicism in 1675, and when she died at age 24, those at her bedside were amazed to witness the terrible smallpox scars disappear

completely from her peaceful face. Many miracles have been associated with this young Mohawk maiden, and now she is a candidate to become the first Native North American saint. And that delicate cupola perched atop the modern Ramada Inn just across from the stone cross, if it looks a bit incongruous, like a dainty historic gazebo somehow swept up by a strong wind and stranded in a later century, that's because it came from the old convent that formerly graced the site, and the act of sale required its preservation.

Naquin's Bed & Breakfast is a favorite stopover for French travelers especially, because both Joyce and Frank grew up speaking Cajun French and in fact did not learn English until they started school. For years they have enjoyed taking in French foreign students studying at nearby Nicholls State University and hosting exchange families from France. Besides giving guided tours to these French visitors, Joyce Naquin made sure her guests got a tasty introduction to Cajun cooking, and pretty soon the guests were begging for recipes and cooking lessons. Thus was born *La Cuisine des Cajuns sur le Bayou,* Joyce's compendium of the best of Cajun cooking, printed with instructions in both English and French for typical local favorites from gumbo and jambalaya to alligator sauce piquante. Guests in the B&B are treated to a good

sampling from the book, often starting off the mornings with alligator boudin and ending with crawfish pie or something equally indigenous to the area.

Joyce was from a big family, and cooking for a group has never fazed her. She says she never did learn how to cook for only 2, and even on her honeymoon, when she set out to cook an intimate little dinner for Frank, she made chili beans using 4 pounds of red beans, producing enough to feed the newlyweds and dozens of their closest friends and family for a week. But that's nothing: Frank is the 15th child in a family of 17 children, and his family's recipe for corn soup began with sending the boys into the field to pick 500 ears of corn to feed the 40 or so hungry mouths when the older siblings brought home spouses and children. The soup was simmered in a big outdoor kettle and eaten with hot homemade bread made in an outdoor oven!

Both the Naquins are now retired, she from nursing and he from naval construction. Frank is an avid fisherman with a camp near the Gulf of Mexico where lucky guests may be taken by special request. Joyce gets into the sport as well, because her recipes for alligator sauce piquante don't start with the sauce piquante, they start with the alligator. Although she admits that in Thibodaux today

you can purchase alligator meat at the supermarket or from a friendly fisherman, Joyce Naquin herself has been on alligator hunts in the wild, and her accounts of wrestling with hissing, flailing 10- or 12-foot gators are so fascinating and so foreign to the experience of most city dwellers that she has printed them up for her guests to enjoy.

Alligators, once considered an endangered species, now abound in the millions in Louisiana, but hunting is still closely monitored and controlled. Some 2,000 licensed alligator hunters harvest about 30,000 alligators annually from the swamps and wetlands, but there is such a demand for alligator products that alligator farming operations supplement those taken in the wild and also collect wild eggs to hatch on the farms, safe from predators, returning at least a portion of the young gators to the wild.

Joyce Naquin says alligator meat has a mild flavor and is easily substituted in recipes calling for veal, chicken, or even most seafood. The recipes that follow, including some of her alligator specialties, are from her cookbook, *La Cuisine des Cajuns sur le Bayou*, now in its 4th printing. She recommends slicing and marinating alligator meat in Italian or Thousand Islands dressing, along with some garlic and wine, to assure tenderness. For her guests' breakfasts, Joyce prepares homemade biscuits with homemade jam or preserves like her persimmon jam shown here, fresh-squeezed juice (this area is tropical enough to grow plenty of citrus fruit), scrambled eggs with ham and cheese, grits, and coffee, sometimes even alligator sausage or boudin.

You can reach Naquin's Bed & Breakfast and order cookbooks by telephoning 985-446-6977, emailing naquinsbb@hotmail.com, or writing 1146 West Camellia Dr., Thibodaux, LA 70301; online see www.naquinsbb.com.

Persimmon Jam

4 lb. (about 10) very ripe persimmons
4 cups sugar

Cut persimmons in half and scoop out pulp. Press fruit through a strainer, put through a food mill, or puree in a food processor. Measure 5 cups pulp into 4½-qt. pot. Add sugar and stir well. Stirring constantly, cook over low heat until thickened, about 30 minutes. Keep the fruit mixture below the boiling point or the jam will become bitter. Remember that the jam will thicken on cooling. Ladle jam into clean, hot jars, leaving ½-inch headspace. Seal. Process in boiling water bath 10 minutes. Yields 3-5 pt.
Recipe from Joyce Naquin.

Beignets

2-3 cups flour
1 tsp. salt
1 tbsp. baking powder
½ tsp. nutmeg
1 cup sugar
1 tsp. soda
4 eggs, well beaten
½ cup water
¼ tsp. vanilla
Oil for deep-frying
Powdered sugar (optional)

Mix dry ingredients. Combine eggs, water, and vanilla. Add to dry ingredients. Mix only until moistened throughout. Knead lightly on slightly floured board. Roll dough ⅓ inch thick. Cut into 2x3" rectangles. Fry in oil until golden brown, turning once. Drain on paper towels. Can be coated with powdered sugar or dipped into cane syrup. Beignets are the Cajun version of homemade doughnuts. Serves 8.
Recipe from Joyce Naquin's Maman Percle.

Hush Puppies

1 cup corn meal
4 tbsp. flour
1 tsp. salt
1 tsp. sugar
1 egg, beaten
3 tbsp. minced onion
1 tsp. baking powder
1 tsp. soda
3 tbsp. shallots
½ cup water
Oil for frying (at least 2" deep in pan)

Combine all ingredients except oil. Drop by teaspoonfuls into hot oil. Fry until golden brown. Hush puppies will turn themselves so that all sides will be browned in 3-5 minutes. Serves 6.
Recipe from Joyce Naquin.

Corn Soup

¼ cup butter
¼ cup flour
2 dozen ears of corn, cut whole kernel style
6 ears corn, whole
2 lb. small shrimp (optional)
1 cup diced tomatoes
½ cup chopped onions
½ cup shallots
⅛ tsp. rosemary
⅛ tsp. sage
½ cup chopped celery
3 qt. hot water
½ cup parsley
2 medium-sized potatoes, cubed
1 cup cooked rice

Make a roux by heating butter in a heavy black iron pot. When hot, gradually add flour, stirring continuously until well mixed. Lower flame and continue stirring until roux is chocolate brown. When brown, add corn, shrimp, tomatoes, onions, shallots, rosemary, sage, and celery. Cook over medium heat, stirring often, until wilted. Add hot water, parsley, and potatoes, and simmer for 1 hour and 45 minutes. Serves 8.
Recipe from Joyce Naquin.

Alligator Sauce Piquante

2 lb. lean alligator, cut in cubes
Salt, pepper, and garlic salt to taste
Worcestershire sauce and Tabasco sauce to taste
½ cup oil
1 bell pepper, chopped
2 medium onions, chopped
1 small can mushroom steak sauce
¼ tsp. sweet basil
1 medium can tomato sauce
1 qt. water
½ lb. fresh mushrooms, sliced and sautéed

Season alligator with salt, pepper, garlic salt, Worcestershire sauce, and Tabasco sauce to taste. Brown it well in just a little oil in a heavy pot. Remove alligator and sauté bell peppers and onions in oil. Return alligator to pot and add mushroom steak sauce, sweet basil, tomato sauce, and water. Add sautéed mushrooms. Simmer over low heat for 2-3 hours. Serves 8-10.
Recipe from Joyce Naquin.

Crawfish-Stuffed Tomatoes

8 large tomatoes (may substitute bell peppers)
½ cup breadcrumbs
½ cup parsley, chopped
½ tsp. salt
½ tsp. pepper
1 clove garlic, crushed
⅛ tsp. liquid crab boil
2 cups crawfish tails, minced
Breadcrumbs or grated cheese for topping
8 tsp. water

Wash and cut off tops of tomatoes and save. Scoop out centers into bowl, leaving shells ⅓-inch thick. Combine remaining ingredients, except that reserved for topping, with tomato centers. Mix well, check seasoning, and fill tomatoes. Place 1 tsp. of water in each cup of a muffin tin. Place stuffed tomato in each. Bake in 350-degree oven 20 minutes or until well heated. Serve with grated cheese or breadcrumbs on top. Serves 8.
Recipe from Joyce Naquin.

Crawfish Pie

¾ cup bell pepper, chopped
1 cup chopped onion
2 cups chopped celery
¾ cup butter
6 tbsp. crawfish fat (optional)
1½ lb. crawfish tails, peeled and chopped
1 cup chopped green onions
½ cup parsley, minced
1 cup shallots
1½ tsp. salt
½ tsp. black pepper
½ tsp. garlic powder
½ tsp. red pepper
⅛ tsp. liquid crab boil
Cornstarch to thicken
2 9" pie shells

Add bell pepper, onion, and celery to butter. Sauté until tender. Add crawfish fat, cover, and simmer 10 minutes. Add chopped crawfish tails, green onions, and remainder of seasonings. Thicken if necessary with a little cornstarch. Place the dough in a 9-inch pie shell. Put filling in one pie shell and using the second shell as crust, place over filling. Place pie in a preheated 450-degree oven and bake for 10 minutes, then lower heat to 375 degrees for 35 minutes or until crust is golden brown. Serve hot as a main course. Serves 8.

Recipe from Joyce Naquin.

Laurel Valley Plantation

In 1905 there were 105 of them still standing. In 1982, when a book was published showcasing all of Louisiana's National Register-listed architectural treasures, there were 76 of them remaining. Now there are only 60 of the original dependencies still standing on Laurel Valley Plantation, nearly half having been lost to the ravages of time and weather over the last century. That, however, is enough to bear mute testimony to the enormity of the labor force and support facilities required to keep south Louisiana's giant sugar plantations running smoothly. And those that are left march through history, their rusted tin roofs slanting uniformly in long rows, their gallery rails cobbled together of bits and pieces of mismatched wood, their steps caving in, the doors to the tiny wood outhouses behind each cabin ajar. But what a poignant plaint echoes through their empty rooms and cold, cold hearths.

Laurel Valley is considered the largest surviving 19th- and 20th-century sugar plantation complex in the country. The workers' quarters stand silent and empty now, machinery having replaced much of the manual labor, but the fertile surrounding fields continue to produce huge yields of sugarcane just as they have done for centuries.

Laurel Valley began in the 1770s when Acadian exile Etienne Boudreaux received 528 acres in a land grant from the Spanish crown. Like most of the small Acadian farmers settling in the area after *le Grand Dérangement* expelled these sturdy French peasants and farmers from Nova Scotia, Boudreaux probably farmed crops like corn, rice, and okra. The 1810 census shows 13 people living on the farm. Not until Boudreaux's death would Laurel Valley's boom years begin.

A young Mississippi planter named Joseph W. Tucker purchased Laurel Valley in 1832, just as

sugar was becoming the white gold that replaced small subsistence farms with highly profitable big plantations. He expanded the plantation to more than 3,200 acres, began planting sugarcane, and built his own sugar mill in 1845, a picturesque arcaded mill of brick considered one of the finest of its kind. He also introduced slave labor, for a huge number of workers were required for such an enormous undertaking.

The sugar industry in south Louisiana was a year-round enterprise, with plowing and planting in January, the slaves guiding mule-drawn plows to make deep grooves in the fields, where seed cane was planted in furrows and covered. By the end of the winter months sugarcane planting was complete; while the cane grew tall in the fields, the labor force planted corn, peas, and other crops. In summer the fields had to be cleared of weeds and brush. Preparations began for the harvest, cutting and stockpiling wood used for fuel in making the sugar and for building molasses barrels and hogsheads to hold the sugar. In mid-October the harvest and grinding season began, with the gangs of cutters using cane knives 2 feet long and 4 inches across, the sharp blades tapering to a narrow hook at the end. Grasping the stalk of cane, the cutter slashed it at the roots with the knife, then ran the blade up the stalk to strip the leaves. The cane was hauled in carts to the sugar house.

Converting sugarcane to raw sugar in the early 1800s was done by animal power, and later steam, and involved a series of 5 steps to grind the cane, purify the extracted juice, evaporate the juice to a viscous syrup, granulate the syrup into sugar crystals, and separate the crystals from molasses by slow drainage. Between the 1820s and the late 1850s, sugar production quadrupled in Louisiana; in 1861 the state produced a record 264,000 tons of sugar. Then came the Civil War, and sugar production in Louisiana dropped precipitously to a mere 9,950 tons in 1865.

At Laurel Valley, the Civil War era brought the death of Tucker and his widow's loss of the property. After the war, Joseph William Tucker's oldest son leased the plantation and ran it with contract labor, even employing 23 Chinese workers in 1871, but he fell further and further in debt. Another of Tucker's sons tried and held on for 2 grinding seasons before he too had to give up. Laurel Valley, sharing the fate of many of the big plantations in

the impoverished transitional years after the Civil War, was sold at public auction.

The plantation rebounded under the ownership of Burch Wormald of New Orleans, who expanded the mill's operations by switching from open pans to the new technique utilizing steam-train vacuum pans and centrifugals to turn the cane into sugar. He also built a dummy railroad system to haul cane from the fields to the mill. Sugar production was increased and cotton was planted, but eventually Wormald too lost Laurel Valley to its mortgage holder. Under the ownership of Frank Barker and J. Wilson Lepine came the real golden years for Laurel Valley. These 2 men expanded operations to include the processing of some 4 million pounds of sugar, with a narrow-gauge railroad linking the sugar fields on their 2 plantations to the Laurel Valley mill, which was enlarged and improved.

More than 350 workers lived in the quarters in these years—in 2-room shotgun houses, Creole double cottages, larger single-family cottages, or the boarding house for bachelors and seasonal laborers, all laid out in the classic cabinscape characteristic of rural Southern plantations a century or so ago. They were surrounded by sugar mill, mill pond, mule barn, and other dependencies.

In the 1880s field hands on south Louisiana sugar plantations often were paid as little as $13 a month, often in script redeemable only at the company store, where big markups generally kept the laborer from ever breaking even. State law forbade moving from plantation quarters until the debt to the store was paid. An attempt at labor organization of the sugar workers led to the Thibodaux Massacre of 1887, when worker strikes during the critical grinding period brought out the state militia and resulted in dozens of deaths.

The Laurel Valley sugar mill closed in 1927, and no workers have lived full time in the quarters housing for decades, but sugarcane is still planted

Wooden Mallet

SUCROSE (SUGAR) ANALYZER

This was a transport board for a plow to go from field to field and back to barn Ca. 1980

MOLD CRETE RM KER

DO NOT TOU

COAL BURNING BLACKSMITH FORGE

on the surrounding acreage by the Laurel Valley Corporation. In 1978 the nonprofit Friends of Laurel Valley was formed to protect the site and direct the rehabilitation of the plantation's support system. Their first project was opening the 1906 Laurel Valley Store, selling crafts and housing an impressive museum collection of 19th-century plantation artifacts from small hand tools and utensils to farm implements and a big old, red 1898 French Woods Model No. 5 pickup truck that cost $380. Besides the continuing quest for funds and operational assistance, the Friends have also repaired other structures: the 1910 schoolhouse with its last lessons still on the blackboard, the church, and a few cabins dating from 1815 to 1877. For now, the Friends are concentrating on maintaining what they have, and public access to the quarters is mainly along the public road that traverses the site, except on guided tours, which must be arranged in advance. The Laurel Valley Store, along Bayou Lafourche on LA 308 east of Thibodaux, is open Wednesday through Sunday; phone 985-447-9351 or write Box 1847, Thibodaux, LA 70302.

Hoe Cakes

1 cup cornmeal
Boiling water
1 tbsp. flour
1 tsp. salt
1 egg, beaten
Milk to make thin batter
Hog lard or bacon drippings

Scald cornmeal with enough boiling water to dampen well. When cool, sift in flour and salt. Add beaten egg and milk to make batter thin. Beat well. Heat griddle until it is very hot and grease well with hog lard or bacon drippings. Spread batter onto griddle and turning once, cook until lightly browned on both sides. Serves 4.

Early plantation workers across the South often used a simplified version of this recipe and instead of a griddle used a hoe blade on which to cook the cornmeal batter cakes over the hot coals of an open fire in the fields. The Nicholls State University professor most involved with the Laurel Valley site, Dr. Paul Leslie, says even the later residents of the quarters were most concerned with work and basic food needs, certainly not anything exotic or fancy, and they ate large quantities of white beans and rice and other simple and inexpensive staples.

White Beans

2 lb. white beans
8 qt. water
1 lb. salt meat, cubed
1 lb. smoked sausage, sliced
4 large onions, chopped
Salt and pepper to taste
¼ cup cooking oil
¼ cup chopped green onions
¼ cup parsley
1 cup shallots

Wash and rinse beans, cover with 4 qt. water, and let soak for 30 minutes. (If beans are not fresh, soak overnight in water and 2 tbsp. soda.) Over medium heat, boil beans until water turns yellow. Remove from heat and drain. Combine beans and 4 qt. of fresh water, add salt meat, sausage, and onions. Cook over medium heat for about 1 hour. When beans start to get soft, add salt and pepper to taste, cooking oil, green onions, parsley, and shallots. Cook for 2 hours or until beans are tender. Serves 10 or more, especially when served over steamed rice to make it go farther.

This recipe from Joyce Naquin serves a lot of people, at least 10, and contains a lot of starch, like most Cajun recipes, because Joyce says that to feed large families on small budgets the cooks had to make the food stretch as far as possible by adding lots of rice and beans.

Rienzi Plantation

Beautiful Spanish-style Rienzi, with its double entrance stairs curving gracefully from ground level to the 2nd-floor gallery, was erected around 1796 for Queen Maria Louisa, consort of King Charles IV of Spain. Built at the time Spain's colonies were slipping from her grasp due to the irrational diplomacy of Charles IV, antagonistic to both France and England, Rienzi was to provide a refuge, a place of retreat in case of abdication.

While Queen Maria Louisa never actually occupied the home, her representative to America, Juan Ygnacia de Egaña, did live there, holding great balls and banquets honoring delegates from the Spanish crown. After Napoleon transferred Louisiana to the United States in the great Louisiana Purchase of 1803, Juan Ygnacia de Egaña purchased the Rienzi property himself and became a successful planter. It was he who planted the grove of immense live oaks whose graceful, swooping branches shade the landscaped grounds today.

Built just across Bayou Lafourche from the little town of Thibodaux, Rienzi in the decade after 1814 was owned by the founder of the town, Henry S. Thibodaux. It is listed on the National Register of Historic Places in recognition of its historical associations as well as its architectural significance as one of very few Southern examples of a plantation house with a cruciform hall plan, 2 intersecting central hallways on each floor making a cross

shape. The lower halls were originally open to the outside through brick archways. The square central core is surrounded by galleries on all sides, with brick gallery pillars on the lower story and wooden posts upstairs.

The Levert family purchased Rienzi in 1896, and the Levert Land Company recently donated the property to the Chef John Folse Culinary Institute at Nicholls State University as an auxiliary campus for use as offices, culinary museum, and a spectacular setting for catered receptions. On the grounds, the Ruth U. Fertel Culinary Arts Building will add additional facilities in honor of the shrewd divorcee who hoped to fund her sons' college education by mortgaging the family home to purchase a steakhouse for $22,000. On her first day in 1965 she sold 35 steaks at $5 apiece, and Ruth's Chris Steak House turned into one of the best steak restaurants in the country, with dozens of franchises worldwide. The examples of Chef Folse and Ruth Fertel surely serve as grand inspiration for budding chefs and restaurateurs studying at the culinary institute.

A lifelong love of Louisiana's rich culinary heritage and a desire to share that with the world has been the basis for an exceptionally diverse and successful career for John Folse, who now gives back by lending his name and expertise to the culinary school dedicated to preserving and promoting the state's indigenous foods and traditional preparation methods. Out of Folse's love for Cajun and Creole cooking, so uniquely Louisianan as to be to cuisine what jazz is to music, was born one of the fastest-growing programs in an increasingly popular state university. The culinary institute now offers more than 40 courses in a demanding curriculum taught by an excellent staff, supervised externships balancing academics with practical preparation by placing students in fine restaurants across the country, and

even opportunities for foreign studies. The courses at the Chef John Folse Culinary Institute run the gamut from culinary history and development and a basic foundation of food preparation to specialized presentations, inventory control, food science, pricing, safe food preparation and storage, banquet preparation, facility design, research and product development, and of course plenty of hands-on slicing, dicing, butchering, rendering, reducing, garnishing, cooking, and eating. Demonstrations are presented by visiting chefs, and the institute offers periodic public dinners and fundraiser spectaculars featuring gourmet meals designed and prepared by students and faculty to fund scholarships and equipment purchases.

And as Rienzi illustrates a bit of Spanish influence in the early architectural and cultural development of Louisiana, so Chef Folse insists that his students explore the influence of the Spanish cuisine and cooking techniques on the dishes of south Louisiana. More than perhaps anyone else, Chef John Folse has a deep understanding and appreciation of all the early influences that have made Louisiana cooking what it is today, a knowledge he imparts to all his students. The popular Spanish dish paella, for example, he calls the one dish that influenced Louisiana cooking more than any other. Paella was the forerunner of what we now know and love as jambalaya, a hearty dish that kept many poor Cajun families from starvation in the early years, when cash money was scarce, supermarkets unheard of, and a meal had to be made from whatever could be caught in the surrounding wetlands or woodlands or grown in the vegetable patch or raised in the family pigpen or chicken yard. Chef Folse, of course, adds his own uniquely Louisiana twist to traditional Spanish paella.

Catfish Paella

½ cup olive oil
1 cup chopped onions
1 cup chopped celery
1 cup diced red bell pepper
1 cup diced tomato
1 tbsp. diced garlic
½ cup andouille sausage, diced
1 cup frozen peas
4½ cups fish stock
4⅞-oz. catfish fillets, cubed
3 cups raw rice
Salt and cracked black pepper to taste
½ cup sliced green onions

Preheat oven to 350 degrees. In a paella pan or other ovenproof baking dish, heat olive oil over medium-high heat. Sauté onions, celery, bell pepper, tomato, garlic, and andouille until vegetables are wilted, approximately 3-5 minutes. Add frozen peas and blend well into mixture. Add fish stock, bring to a rolling boil, and reduce to simmer. Add cubed catfish, stirring once. Add rice and season to taste using salt and pepper. Blend in sliced green onions. Cover pan with aluminum foil and bake 45 minutes to 1 hour. Remove from oven, stir, and allow to set 30 minutes before serving. Serves 6. Recipe from Chef John Folse.

Chicken Paella

1 3-lb. fryer
Salt and cracked black pepper to taste
Dash of Louisiana Gold Pepper Sauce
½ cup olive oil
½ cup diced onions
½ cup diced celery
½ cup diced red bell pepper
½ cup diced green onions
¼ cup diced garlic
½ cup sliced mushrooms
½ cup ham, diced
½ lb. andouille sausage, sliced
1 cup black-eyed peas, cooked
1 cup tomatoes, diced
3 cups long-grain rice
4 cups chicken stock
1 tsp. dry thyme
1 tsp. dry basil

Cut chicken into serving-size pieces and season well using salt, black pepper, and Louisiana Gold. Set aside. In a 4-qt. Dutch oven, heat olive oil over medium-high heat. Brown chicken well on all sides, a few pieces at a time, until all are done. Remove and keep warm. In the same oil, add onions, celery, bell pepper, green onions, garlic, mushrooms, ham, andouille, black-eyed peas, and tomatoes. Sauté 3-5 minutes or until vegetables are wilted. Add rice and stir-fry into the vegetables for 3 additional minutes. Add chicken stock, thyme, and basil. Season to taste using salt, pepper, and Louisiana Gold. Bring to a low boil and cook for 3 minutes, stirring occasionally. Add chicken, blend well into rice and vegetable mixture, and reduce heat to very low. Cover pot and allow rice to cook 30-45 minutes, stirring at 15-minute intervals. Serves 6. Recipe from Chef John Folse.

Paella Salad

1 7-oz. pkg. yellow rice, cooked
2 tbsp. tarragon vinegar
⅓ cup oil
⅛ tsp. salt
Black pepper to taste
Worcestershire sauce to taste
⅛ tsp. dry mustard
¼ tsp. Accent
2 cups cooked chicken, diced
1 cup boiled, shelled shrimp
1 small can green peas
1 large tomato, chopped
1 bell pepper, chopped
½ cup minced onion
½ cup celery, thinly sliced
1 tbsp. chopped pimento

Mix hot rice, vinegar, oil, and seasonings. Cool to room temperature. Add remaining ingredients. Toss lightly and chill. May be prepared the night before serving. Serves 6-8.
Recipe from Eleanor Young.

Wetlands Acadian Cultural Center, Jean Lafitte National Park

L'Acadie. *Le Grand Derangement. L'Heure de la Honte. Le Cajun chic.* To understand the progressions of Louisiana's Acadian population, the Cajuns, it is necessary to share some of their trials and some of their tribulations, some of their joy and some of their heartbreak, for nowhere in this country is there such a unique culture centering around such a unique group of people. Like south Louisiana itself, always in a state of flux as land is built up by the sediments drained from the entire center of the country and then eroded, so our cultures ascend and then, due to a wide variety of circumstances and influences, recede, and then are rebuilt. The Acadians of south Louisiana have ascended to the heights and plumbed the depths, through it all struggling to hold onto their own traditions and culture. They succeeded beyond their wildest dreams, but it was a wonder that they succeeded at all.

Nowhere can a visitor gain a more comprehensive understanding of this progression than at the Wetlands Acadian Cultural Center in Thibodaux, appropriately situated right on the banks of Bayou Lafourche, for after all the bayou was the center of life in the old days and in many respects it still is. The center is part of the Jean Lafitte National Historical Park and Preserve, a series of 6 sites preserving significant resources in Louisiana's Mississippi River Delta region and exploring Acadiana through a variety of interpretive centers tracking the spread of Acadian settlement in Louisiana from the bayous through the wetlands to the prairies.

The Wetlands Acadian Cultural Center functions as a theater and gallery setting for musical performances, art exhibits, and demonstrations of such early skills as duck carving, net making, boatbuilding, and others of both cultural and economic

importance along the bayou. The center also offers films and ranger-guided boat trips along Bayou Lafourche to historic sites. But the permanent exhibits, the fixed explanatory texts and vintage photographs, are themselves compelling lessons in a history often written in tears.

It was in 1604 that groups of French peasants settled along the Canadian coast at L'Acadie, later called Nova Scotia, escaping rampant disease and both political and religious disturbances in their homeland. Under the Treaty of Utrecht, L'Acadie was ceded in 1713 to Britain, and an attempt was made to force the French farmers and fishermen to swear loyalty to that country. When most of them would only promise not to bear arms against her, they were considered French neutrals in an uneasy truce that lasted 4 decades.

In 1755 came *Le Grand Derangement,* hardly the proudest hour of the British empire. Uneasy because of war with France, England expelled thousands of Acadians, tearing families apart, forcibly isolating the men from their dependents, burning their villages, seizing their properties, and crowding them into unseaworthy ships bound for British colonies in America and the Caribbean, as well as England and France. Many of the Acadians died on these desperate voyages; others disembarked only to immediately begin quests to reunite with their loved ones. Only a poet like Longfellow in his epic *Evangeline* could begin to convey the wrenching heartbreak.

Beginning in 1765, ten years after the Great Upheaval—ten years of poverty, slavery, exile, and contempt—a number of these deportees arrived in the Bayou Lafourche area, and for several decades they were joined by others as word spread of a land where their native French was spoken and the farmland was as fertile as in L'Acadie. The final 7 shiploads arrived in New Orleans in 1785 from France, bringing the number of Acadian refugees in Louisiana to nearly 4,000. Some of these Acadians received stakes from the Spanish government to get started. They adapted their skills to their new environment, and soon small farmsteads sprang up along the river and the connected bayous, the simple raised cottages surrounded by rustic picket fences, the small gardens productive in these fertile floodplains, the yards soon teeming with stair-step children by the dozens.

The spring flooding along the Mississippi deposited nutrient-laden silt along the banks, creating rich, high land for farming; the farther away from the water's channel, the finer the silt, leaving the backlands swampy and not easily plowed or cultivated. Naturally the river frontage lands were most desirable for antebellum plantations once slave labor and an improved process for turning cane syrup into sugar made the raising of sugarcane unbelievably profitable. And so the small subsistence farmers, *les petits habitants,* were displaced by the capital-intensive slave-based plantation system raising innumerable acres of staple crops, and the Acadians spread out along Bayou Lafourche and other former channels and distributaries of the Mississippi, into the swampy backlands.

By the mid-1800s some of the Acadians had become fishermen along the coast during the summers and hunted waterfowl or trapped furbearing animals in the marshes during the winter; some became moss pickers and lumbermen. They lived off the land and did what they had to do to feed their families, and if the game warden had more than a passing acquaintance with them, so be it.

Into *la chaudière,* that trusty old black iron pot, went the oil and flour to make a roux, and onions, bell peppers, garlic, and whatever could be caught or trapped or shot. It made a mighty tasty meal, regardless of what it had started out as.

When the railroads connected the New Orleans markets with the prairies and Bayou Teche in the 1880s, the Acadians spread out even farther but remained concentrated mostly across some 22 parishes of south Louisiana. It was inevitable that they would eventually be defined by cultural and linguistic isolation as much as by location and livelihood.

Often ridiculed, persecuted, and misunderstood, the Cajuns tenaciously clung to their traditions, speaking a French that became increasingly their own. If the British had treated them abominably in

L'Acadie, their new American neighbors were hardly models for tolerance in the 19th century. In 1916 the Louisiana Board of Education forbade the use of French in schools in a misguided attempt to force the Acadian children to learn English. L'Heure de la Honte, the time of shame, would not end until a few farsighted politicians and educators began to sponsor French educational and cultural programs and exchanges. By the 1950s there appeared a renewal of Cajun pride that began tentatively in the bayous and soon swelled into a national appreciation for the joyfully unique music, dancing, cooking, and culture, the joie de vivre that refused to be extinguished. The Hour of Shame was replaced by Cajun Chic, and the fascinating exhibits in the Wetlands Acadian Cultural Center take the visitor along every step of the way.

Smothered Rabbit

1-2 wild rabbits, cut in pieces
Season-All to taste
Cayenne pepper to taste
1 tbsp. flour
½ cup oil
8 oz. can cream of mushroom soup
Water to cover
4 medium onions, chopped
2 medium bell peppers, chopped

Season rabbit with Season-All and cayenne pepper. Lightly coat with flour. Heat oil in black iron pot. Slowly add rabbit to hot oil. Brown until rabbit sticks to pot. Add soup and stir well. Cook for 5 minutes. Add water to cover most of rabbit. Stir well. When water boils, add onions and bell peppers. Cover pot and slow cook until rabbit is tender. Serve over rice. Serves 8-10.
Recipe from Spuddy Faucheux.

Smoked Coon Gumbo

1 large smoked coon, cut in small pieces
2 gal. water
1 cup oil
1 cup flour
Beef base, optional
1 lb. smoked turkey necks, optional
½ lb. andouille, cut up
1 lb. smoked sausage
1 lb. chicken gizzards, optional
1 clove garlic, chopped
Salt to taste
Black or red pepper to taste

Boil coon in water until tender, reserving water for stock. Remove coon from water and set aside. Create roux by combining oil and flour and cooking until light brown. Add roux a little at a time to boiling stock until stock is a little thicker than soup. If using beef base and turkey necks, add to stock now. Let simmer about 30 minutes. Add andouille and let slow boil for 30 minutes. Add sausage. Slow boil for 20 minutes. Taste turkey necks; if they are tender, add coon. Slow boil an additional 10 minutes. The smoked meat will season the gumbo, but garlic, salt, and pepper can be added to taste. Serve over rice. Freezes well. Serves 8-10. Recipe from Spuddy Faucheux.

Pouledeau (Poule d'Eau) Gumbo

3 pouledeau breasts
6 pouledeau gizzards
Roux
2 tbsp. beef base, optional
1 lb. smoked turkey necks, optional
1½ lb. andouille, cut up
1½ lb. smoked sausage
1 clove garlic, chopped
Salt to taste
Black or red pepper to taste

Boil pouledeau breasts and gizzards in water until tender, reserving water for stock. Remove from water and set aside. Add roux a little at a time to boiling stock until stock is a little thicker than soup. Add beef base and turkey necks. Let simmer about 30 minutes. Add andouille and slow boil for 30 minutes. Add sausage and slow boil for 20 minutes. Taste turkey necks; if they are tender, return pouledeau and gizzards to the pot. Slow boil for 15 minutes. The smoked meats will season gumbo; add garlic, salt, and pepper to taste. Serve over rice. Freezes well. Serves 8-10. Recipe from Spuddy Faucheux.

Deer Sauce Piquante

½ cup oil
5 lb. venison, cut in bite-size cubes
1 gal. water
1 cup flour
1 cup oil
Small can tomato sauce
20 oz. V-8 juice
1 clove garlic, chopped
1 6-oz. can sliced mushrooms
1 medium jar black olives, optional
Season-All
Cayenne pepper
Salt

Heat oil in black iron pot, add deer meat, and sauté 20 minutes. Add water and bring to boil. Create roux by heating flour and oil until brown. Add roux slowly to stew until consistency of thick soup. Cook 30 minutes over low fire. Add tomato sauce, V-8 juice, garlic, mushrooms, black olives, Season-All, cayenne pepper, and salt. Stir well. When water boils, lower fire, cover pot, and simmer 1 hour. Taste and adjust seasonings. If sauce piquante is too thick, add a little water; it should have consistency of thick soup. Serve over rice. Make this dish when you have time; the longer you cook it, the better it is, so allow at least 3 hours. Serves 8-10. Recipe from Spuddy Faucheux.

Smothered Turkey Necks

5 lb. raw turkey necks
Season-All to taste
Granulated garlic to taste
Cayenne pepper to taste
Accent to taste
1 tbsp. flour
Oil to cover bottom of pot
Water to cover
2 medium onions, sliced
2 medium bell peppers, sliced

Season turkey necks with Season-All, garlic, pepper, and accent. Lightly coat with flour. Cover bottom of black iron pot with oil. When oil is hot, brown turkey necks, turning every 2-3 minutes. Don't let them stick. When they begin to blacken, cover ¾ with water. Cover with onions and bell pepper. Bring water to a boil. Lower fire for turkey necks to cook on low boil; this will make your gravy. Cook until meat is tender enough to be pulled off the bone. Turkey necks and gravy may be served over rice or pasta. Serves 8-10.

Recipe from Spuddy Faucheux, who says not to laugh at this dish. It is easy and delicious and can even be cooked in a slow cooker while the chef takes a long, long nap.

The Culinary Herpetologist

The bousillage that insulated the tiny Cajun cabins along the bayou was made of mud, moss, deer hair, and just about everything else that didn't jump out of the way and run for its life when the plaster was being mixed. A similar recipe was followed by the thrifty Cajun cooks for the rich stews and spicy gumbos bubbling in black iron pots on the hearths of these same little cabins, with native herbs and seasonings jazzing up the coons or crabs or whatever could be trapped, caught, or shot to put food into the mouths of the dozens of hungry children. In other words the cookbook called *The Culinary Herpetologist,* would have been right up their alley.

Hint: Herpetology is the branch of zoology dealing with reptiles and amphibians, a field of study not normally associated with the culinary arts. But octogenarian author Ernest A. Liner of Houma sees nothing incongruous about combining the two, noting that reptiles have been and continue to be eaten by many human cultures around the globe. Not that he recommends rushing out to throw an endangered salamander into your soup, but he has collected 950 reptile and amphibian-based recipes ranging from alligator Pointe-Aux-Chênes to iguana fricassee, from Blackfeet Indian jellied snake to roasted poison-dart frog from the historic Campa Indians of Peru. Admiring colleagues call Liner's amazing book much more than a compilation of curiosities and oddities, but rather a scholarly work with considerable cultural and historical value.

Ernest Liner recalls getting in trouble for catching his first snake, a copperhead he pinned down

106

with a stick and captured in a milk bottle with a potato stopper, on a Cub Scout field trip at age 8. Now he is a respected expert in the field, having conducted extensive research trips throughout the United States, Mexico, Honduras, and Costa Rica. He has discovered new species, published dozens of scientific papers, and is still working on cataloguing the herpetofauna of Mexico. The University of Colorado at Boulder awarded him an honorary doctorate of science in recognition of the importance of his contributions in the field.

So the next time you get a hankering for fried bullfrog tadpoles, *The Culinary Herpetologist* is the answer to your prayers and may be ordered from Bibliomania! at P.O. Box 58355, Salt Lake City, UT 84158-0355; telephone 801-562-2660.

Rattlesnake Creole

1 medium rattler, dressed
¾ cup plain flour
Salt and pepper to taste
Paprika to taste
¼ cup butter
1 4-oz. can mushrooms, sliced; reserve liquid
1 cup white wine
1 8-oz. can tomato sauce
½ tsp. ground basil
4 chicken bouillon cubes
1 onion, diced
2 bell peppers, diced
¼ cup cornstarch
¼ cup water

Clean meat from bones and cut into bite-size pieces. Season flour with salt, pepper, and paprika. Dredge meat in flour and brown in butter. In a saucepan combine mushroom liquid, wine, tomato sauce, basil, and bouillon; simmer 15 minutes. Stir in mushrooms, onion, peppers, and meat. Cover and cook over low heat for 30-45 minutes or until meat is tender. Combine cornstarch and water, and stir into creole until thickened. Serve over rice. Serves 4-6, depending on the size of the snake, of course.

Gator Jambalaya

1 medium onion, chopped
1 cup celery, chopped
1 stick butter
2 lb. alligator meat, cooked and diced
4 cups chicken or alligator broth
1 cup raw long-grain rice
1 4-oz. can mushrooms, sliced
1 clove garlic, minced
2 tsp. salt
1 tsp. Tabasco sauce
1 scallion, chopped
1 cup chopped parsley

Sauté onion and celery in butter until soft and then add the meat, broth, rice, mushrooms, garlic, salt, and Tabasco sauce. Bring to a boil. Simmer 15 minutes, then add the scallion and parsley. Cover and simmer 15-30 minutes, stirring occasionally. Serves 6-8.

Alligator Grillades

1 lb. alligator tail
1 tbsp. plain flour
¼ cup olive oil
½ medium onion, minced
1 red bell pepper, minced
1 stalk celery, minced
1 tsp. garlic, minced
4 sprigs parsley, chopped
1 16-oz. can Italian plum tomatoes
3 leaves basil, chopped
½ tsp. salt
¼ tsp. white pepper
⅛ tsp. cayenne pepper
¼ cup dry white wine

If possible use meat from a young alligator and cut the cutlets against the grain about ¼" thick. Tenderize if necessary. Lightly dust the cutlets with flour seasoned with a little salt and white pepper. Heat the oil in a skillet until almost smoking and sauté the cutlets for about 1 minute on each side. Remove and keep warm. In the remaining oil sauté onion, bell pepper, celery, garlic, and parsley until tender. Chop tomatoes and add them to the skillet along with tomato juice, basil, salt, pepper, cayenne, and wine. Bring to a simmer and return the cutlets to the pan. Cook them in sauce for 5 minutes. Serves 6-8.

The Houma Indians of Bayou Country

French explorer LaSalle, claiming Louisiana and the Mississippi River valley for France, first mentions the Houma Indians living along the banks of the Mississippi in 1682. Chevalier Henri de Tonti found the "Oumas tribe, the bravest of all the savages," and in 1699 Iberville also met the great *"Chef des Oumas."* But when he revisited the Houma village the following year, he found that nearly half the tribe had perished of *"la maladie du flux de ventre,"* dysentery. The introduction of diseases against which they had no immunity, especially smallpox, was only the first of a long line of disservices done the Native Americans by the arriving white men.

Houma means "red" in Choctaw, and it was the Houmas' boundary mark of their hunting grounds, a red stick or pole decorated with fish heads and bear bones, that gave Louisiana's capital city of Baton Rouge its name. The name of the tribe apparently comes from a shortened form of their original tribe, the Chakchiuma, or red crawfish, from which the Houmas separated in the late 1600s. The Houmas continued to use a red crawfish as their war emblem, but they more frequently utilized their pledge of peace, an eagle's tail, often migrating to avoid tensions.

From the mouth of the Red River down to the Angola region then south toward Donaldsonville, the Houmas were pushed, sometimes by fiercer Indian tribes like the Tunicas, sometimes by white migration. They established the village called Chufahouma where the city of Houma is located today, settled along Bayou Terrebonne and Little Caillou, then ended farther south in the coastal marshlands around Bayou DuLarge, Dulac, Isle Jean Charles, Golden Meadow, and Pointe aux Chenes. Their chief in 1859 had managed to purchase a large area of swampland for the tribe, but the discovery of oil and gas there led to yet another

expulsion for the Houmas, many of whom spoke only French and could neither read nor write.

Each move required adaptations and adjustments by the Houmas, who historically were settled farmers with a well-developed culture in which religion, music, dance, art, and sports like the ball game *chungke* played major roles. Their villages originally consisted of wattle-and-daub mound

Charles in 1909 was said to have wiped out much of their rich farmland, fine fields of rice, corn, and greens, and so these traditional farmers had to turn more and more to the bayous, swamps, and marshes for their food and livelihoods, becoming expert hunters and trappers. They were also recognized as some of the finest fishermen around. One who came often to fish with them was country music legend Hank Williams, and local lore holds that he wrote his famous song about jambalaya and crawfish pie in Pointe aux Chenes.

Over the years the Houma chiefs have been both men and women, and in fact one of their most revered leaders was Rosalie Courteaux, a fiery woman who led the final southern migration of the tribe and fearlessly defended her people. The tribal chairwoman today is another strong woman named Brenda Dardar Robichaux, who has worked for Indian education for decades.

Even in this century the Houmas have had to fight for recognition and basic rights. Their children were not allowed to attend segregated public schools, and it was not until the '30s that some substandard Indian schools were finally opened, with a 7th-grade cap on Indian education and problems with language barriers and uncertified teachers. Not until 1963 were the Houma children admitted to public schools.

There were other struggles over trapping rights and land ownership and usage. Even the Bureau of Indian Affairs has been slow in recognizing the Houmas, thus denying them federal services. In 1979 the United Houma Nation (UHN) was formed, consolidating 2 Houma tribes, both of which are recognized by the State of Louisiana. The UHN Tribal Council is the governing body for some 15,000 tribal members constituting Louisiana's largest Indian tribe, and it meets regularly to fight for the rights of the Houmas and to preserve their culture.

When the Houma Indians migrated into the south Louisiana area, they brought with them skills as farmers, *traiteurs*, craftsmen, and cooks, and these skills they shared with their neighbors, especially the Acadian exiles who were suddenly faced with having to wrest from unfamiliar swamps and marshlands the means of living and supporting large families. The Indians showed them how to use the native plants in cooking and in healing and also introduced the Cajuns to the rich bounties of the bayou country: wild ducks and geese, small game like

dwellings encircling central public areas, where sacred fire burned in the temple. They planted maize, beans, squash, and melons, and they also hunted and fished. In the early days they wore their hair long and their breechcloths or skirts short, and they decorated their faces and bodies with extensive tattoos, sometimes even flattening their heads.

As their numbers were thinned by disease, massacre, and the early British slave trade, they often joined forces with their neighbors as a means of survival, absorbing members of other Indian tribes. Later in south Louisiana they sometimes intermarried with their Cajun or black neighbors and also, according to at least some sources, with members of Jean Lafitte's band of pirates who from time to time had to hide out in the isolated Indian settlements. Along the way the Houmas' Muskogean language was supplanted by Cajun French, but as a people they remained unusually tall, with readily noticeable features like prominent cheekbones.

As the lands to which they were pushed became poorer and less suitable for farming, they turned more to the marsh for support. A hurricane's tidal wave striking the Indian community of Isle Jean

squirrel and rabbit, white-tailed deer, game birds, and wild turkey. Often the Indian hunters sold their wild ducks and other game in New Orleans, and excellent guides that they were, they helped their Cajun neighbors learn to hunt or trap to supplement the seafood caught in the surrounding wetlands. Says Kirby Verrett, past chairman of the Tribal Council of the United Houma Nation,

> Even today, we share what we've got, and back when the Cajuns came and the Indians helped them, it was another Thanksgiving, this time in south Louisiana. People think gumbo is just Cajun, but it's not; Indian gumbo goes back much earlier, to the days before metal-pot cooking. The early Indians cooked gumbo in a leather pouch, heated with cooking stones of baked clay. And the gumbo was made with wild onions and whatever chicken or seafood we could catch. It was not spicy like Cajun gumbo but emphasized the delicious taste of the natural foods.

When early Louisiana writer Harnett Kane visited the isolated Houma settlement of Isle Jean Charles

more than half a century ago, he had to travel by boat in order to chat with the aged chief, and while there, he observed open fireplaces with heavy iron pots full of gumbos of shrimp and crabs and game.

Today not just older tribal members but younger ones as well recognize the importance of preserving their heritage and passing down an appreciation for their traditional skills. Kay Bergeron demonstrates the making of file at various festivals; as she says, someone needs to pick up the torch and carry it in this fast-paced world of computers. Kirby Verrett and his wife demonstrate authentic Houma cooking, simple and traditional indigenous foods like baked fish with sassafras leaves. Good opportunities for visitors to learn more about Indian heritage are the Calling of the Tribes Pow-Wow at the Grand Bois park in Bourg in March and the Native Village and traditional food booth at the New Orleans Jazz and Heritage Festival in late spring. There is also a special Indian mass at Holy Family Catholic Church on Grand Caillou Road in Dulac to which celebrants wear Native American

clothing. It is held on the Friday night before the July 14 feast day of the Blessed Kateri Tekakwitha, who may soon become the first Native American saint. The mass begins with a drumbeat instead of church bells ringing and ends with an Indian dance.

The Houmas lived close to nature and had a great respect for the healing power of plants. The Indian healer, called the *traiteur* or *traiteuse,* was skilled in curing ailments using only indigenous plant life accompanied by chants, rituals, and prayers. Here are a few of the Houmas' favorite medicinal plants and their uses as curatives.

The leaves of the sassafras tree to which the Indians introduced the Cajuns were ground during the full moon and used to flavor and thicken gumbo, but the Indians valued sassafras's healing influence on the body's metabolism and also used it to ease the fever of measles or chickenpox.

June peach was used for treating intestinal worms.

Elderberry was used for sore joints or sunstrokes.

Sweet bay was used for chills and colds or congestion.

Pokeweed was found to ease the problems of skin diseases, boils or rheumatism.

Basil was good for stomachache.

Prickly ash helped toothaches or sore throats.

Live oak eased dysentery.

Sweet gum was considered effective for treating wounds or ulcers.

Spanish moss from the sweet gum tree eased chills and fever, while moss from the live oak helped the pains of arthritis and rheumatism.

Historic Southdown Plantation House and the Terrebonne Museum

Just off busy Louisiana Highway 311 and engulfed as it is now by the suburban sprawl of bustling Houma, it's hard to envision Southdown Plantation as it was in its heyday, surrounded by thousands of acres of prime productive cane fields, with its own sugar mill and even its own racetrack. But if ever there were a house that symbolized the significance of the sugarcane industry in south Louisiana, this is it; it's called the "house that sugar built."

Like King Cotton on the river plantations north of Baton Rouge, sugarcane had the power to make or break many a planter in the flat bayou country to the south, and the cane industry nurtured Terrebonne Parish from its infancy. The location was propitious, with so many bayous and waterways and canals meeting in Houma that it was called the "Venice of America." The Minors of

Southdown helped start the sugar industry there, sustained it through difficult times, shared the cultural advantages of its prosperous periods, and revitalized it when disease sounded its death knell. Times change, though, and in a parish that once had nearly 90 sugar mills, the Southdown mill was the last one operating until it too was shut down, dismantled, and shipped to Guatemala. Contributing to the demise of sugar mills all across south Louisiana were such factors as the increasing conglomeration of the refining business, shortage of seasonal workers, and conversion of cane fields to soybean production or subdivisions.

The Minor family lost Southdown during the lean years of the Depression, when the extensive sugar operation was being run by the last of the Minor sisters, Mary Minor and her husband, David Pipes, and Margaret Minor and her husband, C. C.

Krumbhaar. The Pipes family lived in the Southdown house until the mid-1930s. After 4 decades of corporate ownership, the house was salvaged in 1975, when Valhi, Inc., a subsidiary of Southdown Sugar, Inc., donated 4.46 acres, the home, and the rear servant's quarters to the Terrebonne Historical and Cultural Society for a public museum and for special events like the popular semiannual arts and crafts festival.

The museum features exhibits both permanent and periodic. Among permanent displays is a bedroom completely furnished with 19th-century pieces belonging to the Minor family, generously donated by Minor descendant Margaret Krumbhaar Shaffer. Other exhibits feature Mardi Gras in Houma, the sugarcane industry in Terrebonne Parish and at Southdown Plantation in particular, the Houma Indians and other Native Americans of the area, a restored 1880s cabin moved from Hollywood Plantation, a collection of porcelains, and photographs, oral histories, and other artifacts illuminating area history and culture.

The Washington, D.C., office of United States senator Allen J. Ellender has been re-created in the Southdown Museum in tribute to a native son who made good. Ellender served 6 terms in Congress from 1936 to 1972, holding responsible positions among distinguished colleagues who held him in high esteem for his work ethic and honesty. But however much he was admired as a statesman, Allen Ellender was revered for something else too. Called "Number 1 in the Senate and Number 1 in the Kitchen," he was a wonderful Cajun cook who learned his culinary secrets at his mother's knee in Terrebonne Parish and enjoyed preparing dishes for presidents and politicians from around the country and around the world; one of the Senate cafeteria's most popular offerings was called Ellender Gumbo. Allen Ellender's recipes were in such demand that he published a small booklet of the most popular ones, samples of which are given below. They all began in the same way, with a rich roux that blossomed into gumbo, shrimp creole, or piquante sauce.

Southdown is open for tours and may be reached by mail at P.O. Box 2095, Houma, LA 70361, by telephone at 985-851-0154, or online at www.southdownmuseum.org.

Pain Perdu (Lost Bread)

1 egg
⅛ tsp. salt
¾ tbsp. sugar
¼ cup milk
3-4 drops vanilla
4 slices bread

Beat egg; add salt, sugar, milk, and vanilla. Pour into shallow dish and drop bread into mixture. Let it absorb as much as possible on both sides. Place slices in well-greased pan and put in hot oven (400 degrees) until dry and brown. Serve with butter and honey. Serves 4.
Recipe from Mary Minor Pipes.

Chicken Pie

1 chicken
3 tbsp. fat
1 onion, finely chopped
Seasoning to taste
1 cup boiling water
2 egg yolks, hard boiled
1 tbsp. butter
1 cup cream
Dash of nutmeg
1 pastry crust

Cut up chicken, removing bones if preferred, and put in deep pot with 3 tbsp. fat. Let brown, then add onion and seasoning to taste. Pour in boiling water, stir well, and let simmer until well cooked. Rub together the hard-cooked yolks, butter, and cream. Add dash of nutmeg. Mix with chicken and pour all into deep pan lined with pastry crust. Put into 400-degree oven and bake until crust is browned. This is an uncovered pie. Serves 4-6.
Recipe from Margaret Minor Krumbhaar.

Basic Sauce

3 slices bacon
3 oz. smoked ham, diced
1 rounded tbsp. flour
2 lb. onion, finely chopped
1 medium bell pepper, finely chopped
1 lemon (use grated rind, then remove white pulp and chop rest of lemon)
3 pods garlic
Few dashes each of Worcestershire sauce, Tabasco sauce, and thyme
2 bay leaves
Salt to taste

Fry the fat out of the bacon; remove bacon from drippings. Fry ham in bacon fat; remove ham scraps. To the fat add flour and brown, stirring constantly to make scorched-tasting "roux." Add onions and fry slowly until well browned and reduced to pulp. Add remaining ingredients at one time and continue to cook slowly for at least 30-45 minutes. If desired, add bacon and ham scraps.
Recipe from Sen. Allen J. Ellender.

Gumbo

2 tbsp. fat
2 lb. okra, diced
Basic sauce
4 lb. shrimp, peeled
2 lb. crabmeat
Water
Onion tops
Parsley

Slowly cook okra in fat, stirring often to prevent scorching or browning, until no longer ropy. Add to basic sauce and continue to cook for not less than 20 minutes. Add shrimp and crabmeat as well as enough water to make the sauce of a soupy consistency. Bring to a boil, reduce heat, and cook for about 20 minutes. About 10 minutes before serving, add a handful of chopped onion tops and parsley. Serve over rice in soup plates. Should be of the consistency of a thick soup.
Recipe from Sen. Allen J. Ellender.

Chicken Sauce Piquante

Basic sauce (if a thicker sauce is preferred,
   make roux with 2 tbsp. flour instead of 1)
1 can tomato sauce
2 cans tomato paste
2 2½-3-lb. chickens, cut in pieces

Thoroughly cook tomato products with sauce. Add chicken and cook until tender. Serve with rice or spaghetti.
Recipe from Sen. Allen J. Ellender.

Candied Grapefruit Peel

1 large grapefruit
Water to cover
1 cup sugar
¼ cup water

Select grapefruit with thick skin. Peel off rind. Boil grapefruit rind in water to cover, changing water 3 times, until rind can be pierced by a straw. Remove from water and drain. Scrape out inner white rind (the pith) and cut outer rind in thin strips. Boil sugar and water to a very thick syrup, add rind, and cook until all syrup has been absorbed. Put on tray and place in the sun to dry, then roll in granulated sugar.
Recipe from Margaret Minor Krumbhaar.

Peach Crisp

4 cups peaches
¾ cup sugar
½ tsp. cinnamon
½ stick butter
1 cup flour

Peel and slice peaches, then cover with half the sugar and all the cinnamon. Cut butter into flour and add the remaining sugar. Put peaches into well-greased baking dish and cover with flour mixture. Bake at 375 degrees for 30 minutes. Serves 4.
Recipe from Margaret Minor Krumbhaar.

Sherry Flip

1 glass sherry (sherry glass)
1 cup milk
2 tsp. sugar
1 egg
1 ice cube
Dash nutmeg

Put all ingredients in shaker and shake well. Strain and top with a dash of nutmeg. Good for the sick.
Recipe from Mary Minor Pipes.

The Minors of Southdown

The Southdown Plantation property began as a 1790s Spanish land grant briefly owned by the legendary Bowie brothers, Jim and Rezin, then purchased in 1828 by William J. Minor. Born in Natchez, Mississippi, but educated at the University of Pennsylvania in his father's home state, William was the son of Stephen Minor. The elder Minor was certainly one of the most influential foreigners in the Natchez District under Spanish rule and was named in 1797 as Gov. Gayosa de Lemos's successor to guide the transition to American power. The entire town of Natchez, in fact, was built on land the Spanish government purchased from Stephen Minor in 1788.

William J. Minor added to the initial Southdown land grant over the years until he had more than 10,000 acres of prime fields, planted first in indigo and then ribbon cane. The switch proved propitious as the market for domestic sugar increased, and the introduction of steam mills combined with the improved techniques of manufacturing granulated sugar to begin a boom period for the sugar industry. Minor began sugar production on Southdown in 1831 with a yield of 36 hogsheads of sugar and 15 years later constructed his own steam-powered cane mill capable of processing his annual output, which generally ranged between 40,000 and 50,000 gallons. In 1853 the plantation yield was up to 937 hogsheads of sugar. Skilled workmen were brought in, a carpenter was hired to operate a newly completed sawmill set up to provide lumber for mill repairs, and a fine brick mason was employed to construct a large bagasse chimney. There were 176 slaves living on Southdown by the 1850s.

Minor was a shrewd capitalist as well as a successful planter, and he worked closely with his New York factor, a relative, to keep an eye on worldwide sugar crops, weather conditions, and markets to determine the propitious time to sell his own crop;

when crops were short in Cuba and the islands and prices were rising accordingly, he would withhold his sugar from the market until the price had reached a pinnacle. He also kept a close eye on political maneuverings, most particularly as they involved sugar tariffs and import controls.

Minor and his wife brought down from Natchez an Anglo-Saxon influence to this predominantly French area. They had 9 children, all but one of them boys. To house his growing family, Minor began the Southdown house overlooking Little

Bayou Black in 1858. The main body of the house was a single story of Greek Revival style, with 2-story wings enclosing a courtyard, and it has been speculated that perhaps the Civil War interrupted construction. (Two Minor sons died fighting for the Confederacy, though William J. Minor and his wife, both with Pennsylvania antecedents and accustomed to lengthy summer travels to fashionable watering holes throughout the northeast, opposed the war). The bricks for the solid walls, nearly 2 feet thick in places, were made in Minor's own kilns, and from his own swamplands he wrested the cypress for the structural members, finishing the lumber in his own sawmill. A racing enthusiast, he also built stables to house his many fine horses. Southdown even had its own railroad lines and bayou barges to transport cane from its extensive fields to the mill.

When William J. Minor died in 1869, his son Henry Chotard Minor and daughter, Katharine Minor, enclosed the courtyard and abandoned Greek Revival simplicity for the more flamboyant Victorian architectural style then in vogue, adding a 2nd story between towering, rounded turrets on each end of the house flanking the simple double-galleried front entrance. The double front entrance doors feature side and overhead panels of glorious stained glass depicting sugarcane scenes, palmettos, colorful native birds, and magnolia blossoms. The broad, arched entrance hall leads to a carved staircase and, beyond, the original formal dining room. Eleven-inch-thick walls and doorways open from the hallway into spacious rooms with 14-foot ceilings and massive fireplaces—the library, sitting room, bedrooms, breakfast room, and turret-topped parlor with curved walls—while upstairs were 12 more rooms, including 6 more bedrooms and a sewing room as well as screened sleeping porches for summer use. A rear 2-story brick structure housed kitchen and servants' quarters. Just beyond that was the sugar mill.

Henry Chotard Minor married Anna Louise Butler. His sister, Kate, born in 1846, never married but was an active participant in the running of the property, taking it over completely upon the death of her brother; she was also one of the Louisiana commissioners to the 1893 World's Columbian Exposition. When she died in December 1923, the Bulletin of the American Sugar Cane League printed a lengthy tribute to her importance in the planting community:

As we scan the history of the sugar industry of Louisiana we find here and there an instance of feminine conspicuity in its practical affairs, but these instances are not numerous, and we believe that the activities and achievements of Miss Kate Minor transcend those of all others of her sex in the story of Louisiana sugar. She was gifted with such poise and intelligence, such administrative ability and such good judgment, such social accomplishments and personal charm that she shone brilliantly in every phase of her environment. As the last survivor of a family circle consisting of 8 brothers and herself, several of the brothers being prominently identified with sugar production in Louisiana, and as the responsible head for a considerable time of very extensive cane planting and sugar manufacturing interests, Miss Kate Minor found a wide field for the exercise of the high order of business acumen that she possessed, and as the chatelaine of one of the most hospitable and typical of Louisiana's old plantation homes she won high place as a gracious and cultured lady.

And in the *New Orleans Times-Picayune* appeared a large photograph and lengthy history of Kate Minor's life, "a life of simple features, unsophisticated motives and direct influences; to be told in the plain language that she used. She cared not for fine words nor fine clothes and turned aside from them," this fine Southern lady who knew great luxury and social connection.

It was under her management that Southdown became what it is today, the greatest agricultural and manufacturing establishment in Louisiana, the pride of the state and a point of pilgrimage for visiting strangers. At the time of the great Columbian Exposition at Chicago, when women were first recognized as eligible for service in great national affairs, she was appointed by Congress a member of the board of lady managers . . . and she was awarded every recognition that could be given by gratitude, and returned to her native state covered with honor and esteem.

Of the 6 children of Kate's brother Henry, only 3 survived infancy; the youngest, Mary Louise Minor, was orphaned as a young girl and was raised at Southdown by her aunt. Mary and her husband, David W. Pipes, along with her sister, Margaret, and brother-in-law, Charles C. Krumbhaar, supervised the extensive sugar operations at Southdown for years, acquiring additional land to bring the family holdings up to some 20,000 acres and installing a modern sugar mill capable of producing 2,000 tons of sugar daily.

When new varieties of cane were necessary to save an industry threatened by mosaic disease, root rot, and recurrent ravages of hurricanes, it was they who established a USDA sugarcane experiment station at Southdown and with manager Elliot Jones promoted and conducted experiments resulting in the importation of the hardy, disease-resistant POJ strain of cane. Seedlings produced on 4 acres at Southdown represented nearly the total supply in the United States, and these were shared with other planters to save the cane industry from complete failure. Southdown also first introduced the practical utilization of bagasse, sugarcane's previously wasted fibrous byproduct, for the manufacture of building board, as well as the carbon filtration process of juice purification.

Besides the historic home and Southdown's impact on the sugarcane industry, the Minor family left another legacy, several receipt books from the 1800s painstakingly written in flowing script and carefully indexed, filled with family recipes and household hints. The time-honored counsel among these pages covers every problem from dressing calves' heads to killing cockroaches with gum camphor, curing baldness by thoroughly wetting the hair once or twice a week with a weak solution of salt water, cleaning ostrich plumes by steaming until damp and then recurling by drawing them over the blade of a blunt knife, and stopping bleeding from an amputated limb using the powder from a ripe puff ball. It explains how to clean black silk with hot coffee strained through muslin, treat burns or scalds with a mixture of wood soot and lard or linseed oil and lime water or even soda and molasses, and remove bullets or other foreign objects from the alimentary tract by coating the stomach with large amounts of pulverized slippery elm taken internally.

Sage advice is given for ridding bedsteads of bedbugs by sweeping them with feathers doused in wine, turpentine, and gum camphor; for making the best whitewash; for curing pork in brine made of rainwater, salt, baking soda, brown sugar, and molasses; and for treating foundering horses with the seed of the jimson weed as a cathartic. Recommendations include using a fresh tomato leaf as a sovereign cure for a bee sting, onions as

good disinfectants in a room where there is a contagious disease, and corsets with whalebones removed as good cleaning cloths. Coarse complexions of many unfortunate girls are attributable to carelessness in changing the underclothing at night, one tidbit opines. More deadly serious is the first-aid advice for coping with yellow fever in this area where epidemics wiped out whole generations at a time: the patient was to be confined to bed beneath a mosquito bar, his room fumigated with sulphur burning in an iron pot, and the cistern for catching rainwater treated with kerosene.

Some of these recipes and household hints are reproduced in a cookbook called *The Good Earth*, published as a bicentennial project and still available in the Southdown gift shop. Here are a few of the more interesting gems taken directly from the original manuscript, exactly as handwritten generations ago, when refrigeration was unknown and meat was smoked or pickled for preservation and no part of the butchered animal was wasted.

The Concord Receipt for Gumbo

Chicken
Black pepper and salt to taste
Okra
Rice

Cut up your chicken, lay it in cold water till the blood is drawn out, fry it to a nice brown color; season it with black pepper and salt; have a large soup-plate full of okra, chop fine, throwing away the heads and tips of the same as they are hard. Always use the long white, it being more tender and better flavored than the other kinds; stir in this with the chicken, and it will partake of the taste and seasoning of the chicken. Fry it a little, and have ready some boiling water, pouring over, say, three quarts, and allow a sufficient quantity to boil away; let all boil down until the chicken becomes perfectly tender, so that it may easily be torn to pieces with a fork. If fried, it requires more pepper and salt, which should be added before it is thoroughly cooked. The gumbo thus made will be very thick. If you do not like it made in this way, do not boil so much, as it spoils all kinds of soups to boil down and fill up again, as many do with cold water, and besides it is never so rich. Have rice boiled tender, but be careful that the grains are separate.

Receipt for Dressing Calf's Head

1 calf's head
Powdered cloves to taste
Marjoram to taste
Pepper to taste
Salt to taste
Butter to taste
Grated bread
Veal meat balls
Gravy
Claret or wine

Have the head nicely cleaned. Put it on to boil, and boil until the bones come out; mince the meat and mix it with powdered cloves, sweet marjoram, pepper, salt, and butter to the taste. Keep the skin unbroken, put it in a deep dish and rub it over with butter, grating some bread on it which will make it brown well. Garnish the dish with forced meat balls made of veal and season them as the head. Make a rich gravy, and add a glass of Claret or Wine to it.

The Concord Receipt for Pickling Pork and Beef

Hog, cut into pieces
Salt
Salt petre
½ lb. brown sugar
Water to cover

Cut up the hog in pieces to suit yourself; then sprinkle it with salt, on a table or board to extract the blood. Hard salt is the best. Fine salt answers very well but it requires more of it. It can remain in the salt for two or three days if the weather permits. Then pack in the barrel, sprinkling salt between every layer, skin side down; then put the pickle on it which is made by dissolving 6 ozs. of salt petre to every one hundred pounds, ½ lb. of brown sugar, add as much water as will cover the pork well.

To Boil Cauliflower

Cauliflower
Salt
Milk to boil
Water to boil

Cut off the green leaves, and look carefully that there are no caterpillars about the stalk; soak in cold water, with a handful of salt in it, then boil them in milk and water and take care to skim the saucepan, that not the least foulness may fall on the flower. It must be served up very white and rather crisp, with sauce, gravy, or melted butter.

Spanish Cream

6 eggs
6 tbsp. loaf sugar
3 pt. milk
1 vanilla bean or peach leaves (optional)
Powdered sugar

Take 6 eggs and 6 tablespoonsful of powdered loaf sugar and beat them well together, then add 3 pints of rich milk. Stir it well with the eggs and sugar. You can add a vanilla bean or peach leaves (a few) to flavour it. Put the mixture into a bell metal kettle and place it on the fire or stove. Stir it all the while and never allow it to boil. Take it off and after it is perfectly cold, sprinkle powdered sugar over the top of the custard (it must be poured into a handsome China dish or bowl) and scorch the sugar with a hot iron.

Magnolia Plantation

Long a productive sugar plantation along the banks of Little Bayou Black between Thibodaux and Houma, Magnolia was purchased shortly after the Civil War by John Jackson Shaffer, whose father, William, was the first of the family to settle in Terrebonne Parish and whose descendants occupy the house today. Two stories with squared columns supporting double galleries with iron balustrades, the Magnolia Plantation home's architectural style has been called modified Greek Revival and features a purity of line pleasing in its simplicity, without undue embellishment. It was built in 1834 by Thomas Ellis, using cypress cut by plantation workers and pegged together with wooden pegs.

The spacious front hallway is dominated by a magnificent rosewood and mahogany curved stairway that was imported from France all in one piece. The unusual stairwell forming the backdrop

for the stairs is a curved alcove in which is set an extremely unusual curved cypress door that for generations has befuddled and amazed admiring experts from around the globe, who have never seen another like it. The curved door remains in perfect condition except for a crack caused when the present occupant struggled to hold it closed against the terrific winds of Hurricane Betsy.

The high ceilings, crowned by elaborate plaster moldings, are 14 feet, their very height contributing to the coolness inside this house in the absence of air conditioning even today. The double parlors to one side of the entrance hall are divided by massive paneled sliding doors and feature twin chandeliers, immense gold-framed mirrors, and white Italian marble mantels. The Ellis's daughter Eliza was married in this lovely setting to Confederate general Braxton Bragg.

That wedding ceremony took place in happier

times. By the Civil War years, Magnolia was commandeered for conversion into a federal hospital, its parlors and hallways echoing with the moans and screams of wounded and dying soldiers. Its expensive furnishings, so carefully chosen and imported all the way from Europe, were wrecked and ruined; the piano was pulled out onto the lawn and used as a feed trough for the troops' horses.

Thomas Ellis was ruined as well, his home ravaged and economic reversals necessitating the sale of Magnolia in 1874 to Capt. John Jackson Shaffer, C.S.A., and his wife, Minerva. Their granddaughter Bessie Shaffer willed the house to the present owner, M. Lee Shaffer, Jr., her great-great-nephew, in 1957, and it remains filled with family treasures like the hand-carved dining room table that comfortably seats 14 and was transported to the bayou country in the 1820s.

The house was set off by a formal garden and a number of dependencies—detached kitchen and servants' quarters, slave wash house of brick and cypress timbers, milk house with underground stream for cooling the dairy products, and underground cistern that kept drinking water cool, insulated by double walls of brick with crushed charcoal between the layers. Magnolia also boasted such progressive features as an underground drainage system that caught rainwater off the roof and channeled it away from the house in long cypress troughs. On the back porch a rare and complete set of 11 slave bells, operated by a series of wires and pulleys, illustrates the plantation system of summoning help. Each servant had a unique bell tone, easily recognizable and distinguishable from all others, indicating who was wanted and where.

When the members of St. Matthew's Guild of Houma first compiled in 1924 a wonderful little cookbook called *De Bonnes Choses a Manger*, Mrs. J. J. Shaffer shared a number of family recipes, some of which are reprinted here. An 8th edition of *De Bonnes Choses a Manger* with all-new recipes was released in 2005 to commemorate the 150th anniversary of St. Matthew's Episcopal Church and may be ordered from P.O. Box 568, Houma, LA 70361.

Philadelphia Ice Cream

½ pt. milk
1 pt. cream
½ cup sugar
1 tsp. vanilla
Peaches, optional

Scald milk and cream, then add sugar. Stir and let cool. When cold, add vanilla and freeze. Scalding gives the dish a velvety texture not found in other creams. Ripe peaches, mashed through a sieve and sweetened to taste, may be added when cream is partially frozen. Serves 4-6.
Recipe from Mrs. J. J. Shaffer.

Ice Cream Wafers

2 eggs
1 cup butter
1 cup Crisco
2 cups sugar
3 cups flour
2 tsp. salt
2 tsp. vanilla
Pecan halves

Combine all ingredients and spread on greased brown paper 1 tsp. at a time. Put half pecan in center. Bake 350 degrees until slightly browned and crisp. Makes about 6 dozen.
Recipe from Mrs. J. J. Shaffer.

Tipsy Cake

4 eggs
2 cups milk
1 cup sugar
Pinch of salt
Sherry wine
1 sponge cake (square and stale)
Almonds, blanched
½ pt. whipping cream
½ tsp. vanilla

Make custard with eggs, milk, sugar, and salt. Cook until thick. Cool and flavor with a little sherry. Pour sherry over cake, enough to moisten. Place almonds on top and pour half the custard over it. Whip cream, sweeten slightly, and flavor with vanilla. Cover cake with cream. The remaining custard may be used when served. May be frozen in electric refrigerator, using all the custard.
Recipe from Mrs. J. J. Shaffer.

Magical Storybook Ardoyne

A fairytale castle filled to overflowing with family treasures, Ardoyne was built around the turn of the century by an adoring husband whose wife, traveling abroad on an extensive trip to restore her ill health, had requested that he build her "a cottage" in her absence. With its soaring 75-foot tower, bays, arches, and an excess of fanciful Victorian gingerbread trim in many different shapes and styles, Ardoyne joyfully stretches into the sky in an architectural exuberance seen nowhere else in Bayou Country.

John D. Shaffer had the house copied from a magazine picture of a castle in Scotland and named it Ardoyne, which means "little knoll" in Scottish. The architect was John Williams of New Orleans, and the carpenters and laborers executed his design during breaks from the sugarcane harvest. Begun in 1897 and completed in 1900, the house was constructed mostly of native cypress and encircled by covered galleries.

The enormous entrance doors open to a 60-foot central hall with beautiful inlaid wood ceiling and walls hung with priceless artworks, including original Gilbert Stuart portraits of family connections George Washington and his stepdaughter Nellie Custis. The formal parlor leads to the octagonal plantation office and through floor-to-ceiling windows onto the screened mosquito porch, where half of one of the early hogsheads used to ship sugar is still clearly marked with the owner's name and that year's harvest.

In the master bedroom are immense 4-post tester beds, a youth bed, and daybed used by the mistress of the house for naps during the day. Another downstairs bedroom has a fine antique tester bed from Southdown Plantation, home of the maternal side of the family of the present owners, wise and wonderful Margaret Shaffer, an artistic,

creative soul who in her 90s is still an outspoken and colorful character, and her daughter, the quiet retired parish librarian.

The dining room is filled with antique silver and china, family pieces all. The gold and white china came from Charles M. Conrad, great-great-great-uncle of the present owner and secretary of war under Pres. Millard Fillmore. In the front sitting room is a courting sofa as well as original Drysdales and English bookcases filled with rare editions. Among the collections are prized handwritten family recipe books from the 1800s, some of the dishes of such enduring quality as to remain family favorites even today. An immense carved staircase

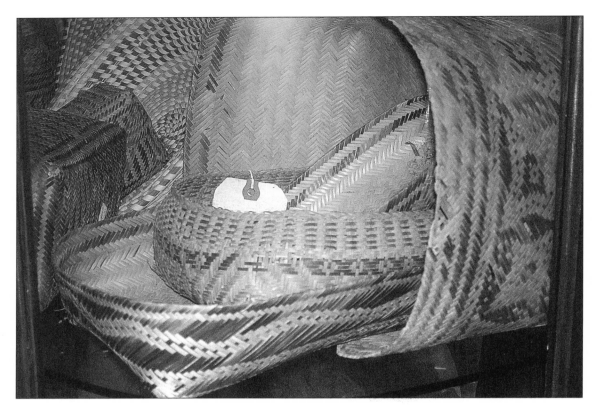

leads from the entrance hall to an upper floor filled with thousands of volumes of rare vintage books and other family treasures. This is a house that has never been sold out of the original family, and so it boasts incredible family collections. Particularly interesting are the large copper lanterns with blown-glass bulbs from the early mule lots, which were used to provide light in the predawn darkness as the mules were harnessed for the day's hard work in the sugarcane fields surrounding the house.

On Highway 311 between Thibodaux and Houma, Ardoyne is a private residence currently occupied by several generations of direct descendants of John D. and Julia Shaffer. Today's owners are ardent preservationists who actively support the cause of salvaging every interesting vestige of history and culture in Terrebonne Parish and the sugarcane industry. Several of their favorite family recipes were used in *Bayou Breezes: A Taste of South Louisiana,* the cookbook of the Junior Auxiliary of Houma, as a fundraiser to support projects benefiting the children of the area. Copies are available from Junior Auxiliary of Houma, P.O. Box 2915, Houma, LA 70361-2915 ($19.95 plus $4 shipping per book).

Sweet Potato Pies

Dough
2 sticks butter, softened
⅔ cup white sugar
1 egg
2½ cups flour
1 tsp. salt
2 tsp. vanilla
2 tsp. cinnamon

Filling
3 sweet potatoes, medium size
1 stick butter
1 tsp. salt
1 cup brown sugar
2 tsp. cinnamon
¼ cup lemon juice

For dough, cream butter and sugar. Add egg and beat well. Add flour, salt, vanilla, and cinnamon. Mix well. Cover dough and chill in refrigerator for 3 hours. Roll dough very thin. Cut into 5-inch circles. For filling, boil potatoes until soft, then peel, put in blender with butter, salt, brown sugar, cinnamon, and lemon juice; blend well. Place spoonful of potato mixture in center of dough circle. Dampen edges of dough with water. Fold and seal with a fork. Bake at 350 degrees for 35 minutes or until golden brown. Serves 15.

Recipe from Margaret Shaffer.

Golden Marmalade

6 oranges, unpeeled
3 lemons
Water to cover
Sugar
1 cup lemon juice

Slice fruit very thin, discarding seed. Cover with water and let stand overnight. Next morning boil fruit and water mixture 45 minutes. Let stand overnight again. In the morning measure and then bring to a boil. Add 1½ times as much sugar as fruit. Boil 45 minutes. Just before removing from heat, add lemon juice. Seal in glasses. Makes 1½ dozen jars.

Recipe from Mrs. M. L. Shaffer.

Molasses

Those of us accustomed to selecting our molasses from the syrup shelf in the supermarket must go back more than a few decades to gain an appreciation of harvest time in sugarcane country, when the narrow winding back roads were strewn with stalks fallen from straining cradle-wagons piled as high as the sky with cut cane being hauled for grinding to immense, pulsating mills belching smoke and deafening noise. The excitement rose to fever pitch among children anticipating a snatched first taste of the sweet yield. In every south Louisiana community surrounded by flat, open fields where interminable, straight rows of tall cane swayed with the breeze and stretched to the horizon as far as the eye could see, there was at least one big co-op mill and usually more than a few small home syrup makers.

In the 1930s, Eleanore Ott of Fair Oaks Plantation in Mount Hermon put together a wonderful little cookbook dedicated to her grandmother Mary Simmons Leggett and published by J. S. W. Harmanson Publisher of 333 Royal Street in New Orleans. Though they are all no doubt long since gone to their great reward, if you ever see this little gem in a used bookstore, snatch it up quick. Mrs. Ott eloquently provides modern-day readers with a real feel for the cooks and outside kitchens of the old days, explaining that if there is any secret to plantation cookery, it is its very lavishness. She cites her grandmother's recipes for cakes containing 20 eggs, chicken fried in real butter, and "one spilling wine-glass of best Bourbon" in the custard pie as examples of what she calls the "fine careless rapture with which the cook tossed in the spirits."

In the vast recesses of the exposed-beam outside kitchen, with its huge open hearth hung with spits and pothooks and 3-legged iron bake ovens among the coals, there were shelves lined with crocks and jars full of preserves and jellies, pickles and canned vegetables, and a churn that held 4 gallons of cream (says Mrs. Ott, "Four gallons of cream! Visualize it if you can, O Reader, ordering your half-pint for very special affairs!"). Outbuildings held barrels of flour and sugar, firkins of green coffee, whole cheeses, root crops, and strings of red peppers, while the smokehouse with its thick pungent hickory smoke was strung with hams and sausages being cured. Close by were herb gardens, vegetable gardens, nesting hens, and a milk house with spring water cooling pans of milk and crocks of butter.

And always there was a much-prized supply of molasses. Mrs. Ott says molasses was to the South what maple syrup was to New England. In pioneer days, she says,

The molasses of the settlers was imported from New Orleans in fifty-gallon oaken barrels. A very thick, almost-black substance it was, too, but high-esteemed by a lover of molasses cookies and cakes—and who wasn't? Later, from the necessities of the War Between the States, the open kettle method of cooking the juice from sugar-cane spread from those vast cane lands, where the planter sent two hundred to a thousand knives out of a chilly winter dawn, to the small upland "cane-patches." Now, when the blue mists of autumn haze the horizon and the peanut-threshers snort like fabled prehistoric monsters, an integral part of the Southern scene is the dottings of smoke from the cane-mills. Here the purple stalks are thrust in a press turned by some plodding patient nag treading a beaten circle and the wine-dark juice flecked with white chaff pours into a vast container. Here under a roof is the furnace covered with flat open vats or kettles, where stand the skimmers with their long-handled ladles, skimming off the grey foam and tossing it aside, hour after hour, while the cane juice bubbles off its rich sweet aroma. When the syrup is thick it is strained and poured into tin buckets. The secret of good syrup, aside from a propitious rich area for the cane-patch, lies in rapid boiling and constant skimming. . . . There are syrups and syrups, from the delicious brown super-excellents down to viscous black tasteless fluids, to syrups that turn to sugar—stirring during the cooking causes that, and while the high moment of a child's life is when he is invited into the kitchen to scrape the rock candy from a syrup can, the cook thinks differently. Most of the so-called Southern syrups on the market are mighty poor imitations of the real thing.

Of course things are a little different nearly a century later, especially regarding the quality of cane syrups and molasses available commercially, with Louisiana's Steen family producing in Abbeville some of the best and shipping it around the world. And of course we miss much of the charm and excitement in the ability simply to stroll the supermarket aisles and select our molasses these days. But some of Mrs. Ott's molasses recipes are still just as good, and a few are given here.

Molasses Cookies

3 cups flour
1 tsp. salt
2 tsp. soda
2 tsp. ginger
¾ cup molasses
½ cup butter
¼ cup vinegar

Sift together dry ingredients. Add molasses, well heated, into which has been stirred butter until blended and vinegar. Stir and beat well. Roll ⅛" thick on floured board. Cut with large cutter and bake on greased baking sheet or cookie pan in hot oven (375 degrees). Do not bake too dry. One winter day when the hens were moulting, somebody concocted this recipe for molasses cookies sans eggs.

Molasses Pie

2 eggs
1 cup sweet milk
1 tbsp. flour
1 tbsp. butter
1½ cups molasses
Dash grated nutmeg
Uncooked pie shell

Beat eggs together. Add 1 teacup of sweet milk, with flour blended into a small portion of this liquid. Add a lump of butter the size of an egg. On the stove have 1½ cups New Orleans open-kettle molasses boiled until very thick—almost to the soft-ball stage. Pour the boiling-hot molasses over the egg mixture and blend thoroughly. Add a dash of grated nutmeg. Bake in a moderate oven (350 degrees) in an uncooked shell. No meringue, please. The whites of the eggs are beaten with the yolks.

Molasses Candy

This recipe comes from an old, undated cookbook sensibly entitled *A Book of Famous Old New Orleans Recipes Used in the South for More Than 200 Years*. Its publisher was Peerless Printing, 515 Lafayette Street, 34th floor, New Orleans, a publisher who cared so strongly that its recipes turn out successfully, and who felt equally strongly that good Creole ingredients were absolutely necessary for satisfactory results, that the foreword included the publisher's address and instructed the cook to write if any requisite ingredients were not readily available wherever in the world that cook might be. The publisher, promised the foreword, would be pleased to procure those. The Molasses Candy recipe, called in French *Candi Tire a la Melasse,* included an introduction insisting that Louisiana was

> rightly the home of Molasses Candy, for it was right here, in this old city, in the environments of which sugar was first raised in the United States, and molasses, sweet and health-giving, was first given to the world, that Molasses Candy, or *Candi Tire* as the Creoles call it, first had birth. Candi Tire parties, or Molasses Candy Pullings, were among the pleasurable incidents of life amongst the early New Orleans belles and beaux.

1 lb. granulated sugar
1 qt. Louisiana molasses
2 tbsp. vinegar
1 tbsp. butter
½ tsp. soda
Juice of 1 lemon
1 tsp. banana extract

Boil sugar until it becomes quite thick when dropped into water. Add molasses, vinegar, and butter; boil until it hardens when dropped into cold water. Stir in small half teaspoonful of bicarbonate soda and pour into buttered tins. As soon as it begins to cool sufficiently, pull until white. Moisten the hands with ice water or butter while pulling. The sticks may be single twisted, braided, or flattened, according to taste. While pulling, add banana extract.

Dat Damn Nutr'a Rat

Sometimes it seems we never learn when it comes to fooling around with Mother Nature. We introduce imported plant and animal life to beautify our surroundings only to find that the foreign invaders upset the delicate domestic balance and devour native species or expose them to diseases against which they have no defense. The ornamental kudzu we so enthusiastically imported from the Orient in the 1870s and touted as erosion control now smothers native trees and shrubs, abandoned buildings, and even napping hound dogs and slow-moving people, if stories can be believed, draping everything in its path as it marches across the South.

The lovely floating water hyacinth, another import generously given away by Japanese businessmen during the 1884 Cotton States Exposition in New Orleans, has proven despite its delicate appearance to be nearly impossible to eradicate and grows so thickly as to choke out waterways and impede boat traffic. So what do we do? We bring in an enormous rodent from South America, the nutria, to eat the water hyacinth. Trouble is, the nutria didn't stop with the water hyacinth. Called "mammalian lawn mowers" by one scientist, these voracious herbivores with their big buck teeth of frightening orange-yellow have devoured everything in their path. Each animal each day can eat an estimated 25 percent of its weight, up to 3 pounds of marsh plants, stems, roots, and all. They are destabilizing the soil base in marshy areas by destroying the root systems of plants, denuding hundreds of thousands of acres of fragile coastal environment, and depleting the food supply needed by other furbearing swamp residents like the native muskrat upon which the trapping industry depended.

Called the coypu in other parts of the world,

nutria are smaller than beavers but larger than muskrats, with adults weighing from 12-20 pounds. They have small forelegs and larger hind legs with webbed feet, and they are considered semiaquatic; they can move quickly across land and can also swim long distances underwater. Nutria have long whiskers and 4"-long dark orange front teeth. Prolific breeders, females reach sexual maturity within 4-8 months and can produce several litters of young every year, with litter size ranging up to 13 babies. The mothers have mammary glands high along the sides of their bodies so the babies can nurse while the mother is swimming through the

water. Nutria have dense undercoats and long, glossy hairs varying in color from dark brown to yellowish; the fur is similar to beaver and has been popular for linings and trims in coats.

There are now millions of nutria in Louisiana, but the problem is not confined solely to this coastal state. Maryland was one of 16 other states with drastic problems after nutria either escaped or were released from a federal fur research project there in 1943. After suffering millions of dollars' worth of economic damage because of reduced opportunities for hunting, fishing, and hiking, not to mention thousands of acres of vanished wetlands along the Chesapeake Bay, Maryland fought back with a trapping program that eliminated more than 8,000 nutria in 2 years. The state first tried a bounty program, but success was attained only by hiring several full-time trappers paid by the hour, not by the animal, to wage continued methodical war against the nutria. Now Maryland's marshlands are starting to sprout bulrush in areas previously left by the nutria as denuded bare mud, and the birds and fish and mammals that live in the bulrush marshes are thriving once more. A similar

incentive-bonus program helped to eradicate nutria in Great Britain in the late 1980s.

It was in the 1930s that nutria imported by fur farms were released into the Louisiana marshes, either accidentally or intentionally, and they have had a devastating effect on Louisiana's coastal wetlands, threatening the stability of the entire fragile ecosystem, damaging levees, ruining sugarcane crops, draining rice fields, and contributing to the decline of the fur-trapping industry. A mere 1,000 trapping licenses were issued in 2001 in Louisiana, where at one time thousands of families made a respectable living harvesting the once-plentiful mink, muskrat, otter, raccoons, foxes, and bobcats in a state once one of the leading fur producers in the country; in the mid-1920s there were over 20,000 licensed trappers. The dramatic drop in fur prices in recent years certainly contributed to the demise of the industry, but ask any old-time trapper and he'll give you another reason: "It's dat damn nutr'a rat!"

In spite of the fact that it took much longer to skin and stretch a nutria pelt than a muskrat, and in spite of the fact that the heavier nutria were

more difficult to transport through the marsh by small pirogue, nutria were successfully trapped for their fur, and after they were skinned the meat was salted down in barrels and used later for shrimp bait. Some 1.8 million pelts worth $15.7 million were harvested in 1976, with demand and prices high enough to provide incentive for trappers, at least until the international fur market dwindled in the late 1980s as fashion trends changed and the market was flooded with European farm-raised products. Reduced trapping made the population of these destructive rodents in Louisiana jump so dramatically that the state-funded Fur and Alligator Advisory Council began efforts to promote nutria fur globally, a program not met with resounding success.

Now the nutria is listed among the top hundred worst invasive species in the world, and the State of Louisiana, after investigating alternatives like poisoning, hunting, and induced infertility, has begun a carefully regulated Coastwide Nutria Control Program offering $4 per nutria tail (with the possibility of also selling the fur and meat) in hopes of encouraging the harvest of up to 400,000 nutria a year; figures for 2003-2005 hover around the 300,000 mark. Failure of this program will mean continued decreases in sport and commercial fisheries production, decreased plant life in the marshes, and an accompanying decrease in habitat areas for other animal and plant life, as well as a lessened ability of the overgrazed marshlands to buffer storm surges during hurricanes. Louisiana's marshland, wildlife biologists warn, will become open water if the nutria population is not dramatically reduced, and soon.

And, oh yes, there was one other balloon floated regarding nutria control. For years, the insider joke in Louisiana was that we should tell the Cajuns, remarkably resourceful and notoriously independent cusses, that the nutria was a protected species and no one should kill or eat them. Famous for creatively adaptive culinary skills born of economic necessity that could turn nearly anything into a palatable meal, even the Cajuns turned up their noses at the nutria. "I don't eat rat," said the less-than-enthusiastic head of the Fish and Wildlife Service charged with promoting the idea in Maryland. The Louisiana response was no doubt

even more colorful but just as positive, although some of the old-time trapping families who spent winters in the marsh living off the land ate not only nutria but muskrat as well.

Professionals were called in. "Nutria meat is surely the most exciting delicacy to come along in years," they said, advertising it under the catchy slogan "Nutria: Good for You, Good for Louisiana." Promoting nutria meat as a cross between dark turkey and rabbit, rich in protein, low in cholesterol, with virtually no fat and no wild-game taste due to the nutria's selective vegetarianism, professional French chef and international food consultant Philippe Parola developed a series of tempting nutria recipes that he insisted were "a major attraction to restaurants, bringing in high praise from customers and food critics alike." The Louisiana Department of Wildlife and Fisheries used grant money under a demo program to fund the development of these recipes, but the funding ran out and the state had a hard time finding a reliable processor to convert the natural product to a form desired by restaurants and chefs. Now the only way to get nutria meat is to run over one on the roadway, unless you know a trapper.

In case you'd like to try a few of these recipes, here are some of the simpler ones; Chef Parola also has fancier ones like Culotte de Ragondin (Nutria) à la Moutarde or Ragondin with Blackberry Demiglace. Consider the consumption your contribution toward conserving Louisiana's marshlands.

P.S.: If you're serving the nutria as your main dish, you'd best consider whipping up some pretty sensational and spicy side dishes, like those provided here. And if all else fails, give the final recipe some serious consideration.

Sweet Hot Jalapeños

1 gal. sliced jalapeños, drained; reserve 1 cup juice
4-5 lb. sugar

Mix reserved jalapeño juice with sugar. Add to jalapeños. Refrigerate for 2 weeks, stirring occasionally. Pack in smaller jars and keep refrigerated. Pour over cream cheese and serve with crackers. Great on hot dogs or sandwiches or with fried fish or chicken. Makes 20 cups.

Recipe from Becky Power, who probably has never tried them with nutria, but they ought to be just the ticket!

Guacamole

5-6 ripe avocados, mashed
1 small onion, chopped
Garlic salt or garlic powder to taste
1-2 tbsp. ascorbic acid (FruitFresh) or lemon juice
Tomatoes or salsa for garnish

Mix well and cover with plastic wrap until chilled and ready to serve. Garnish with chopped and drained fresh tomatoes or salsa. Serve with tortilla chips. Serves 4-6.

Recipe from Becky Power.

Special Green Beans

3-4 cups green beans
Salt and pepper to taste
Onion, chopped, to taste
1 stick butter
1 cup pecans, finely chopped
1 cup breadcrumbs
3 tbsp. brown sugar

Prepare green beans, either canned, frozen, or fresh, and season with salt, pepper, and chopped onion to taste. Drain well and pour into serving dish or casserole. To make topping, mix butter, pecans, breadcrumbs, and brown sugar in skillet over low heat until lightly toasted, stirring constantly to avoid scorching. Cover green beans with topping.

Recipe from Becky Power.

Corn Salad

3-4 cans vacuum-packed whole kernel corn, drained
1 medium onion, chopped
1 medium green pepper, chopped
1 8-oz. pkg. shredded cheese (4-cheese Mexican blend, Colby/Monterey Jack, or taco seasoned)
½ cup salad dressing or mayonnaise
Salt and pepper to taste
1 bag corn chips

Mix until blended all ingredients except chips. Chill until ready to serve. Before serving, mix in slightly crushed corn chips (the chili-cheese-flavored ones are the best). Serves 8-10.

Recipe from Becky Power.

Nutria Sauce Piquante

2 cups margarine
¾ cup flour
3 onions, chopped
1 bell pepper, chopped
2-4 cloves garlic, minced
3 lb. diced nutria meat
1 cup sherry wine
2 cups water
1 cup tomatoes, drained and quartered
½ cup jalapeño peppers, drained

In a large Dutch oven, make a medium-brown roux using margarine and flour. Add onions, bell pepper, and garlic. Cook until tender. Add nutria meat, sherry, and water. Cook on low heat approximately 1½ hours or until meat is tender. Add tomatoes and jalapeño peppers. Cook 30 minutes. Serve over rice with garlic bread. Serves 6.
Recipe from Chef Philippe Parola.

Heart-Healthy Crockpot Nutria

1 small onion, sliced thin
1 tomato, cut into big wedges
2 potatoes, sliced thin
2 carrots, sliced thin
8 Brussels sprouts
2 hind saddle portions of nutria meat
Salt and pepper to taste
2 tsp. garlic, chopped
½ cup white wine
1 cup water
1 cup demi-glace, optional

Layer onion, tomato, potatoes, carrots, and Brussels sprouts in Crockpot. Season nutria with salt, pepper, and garlic, and place nutria over vegetables. Add wine and water, set Crockpot on low, and let cook until meat is tender, approximately 1½ hours. Garnish with vegetables and demi-glace. Makes 4 servings.
Recipe from Chef Philippe Parola.

Baked Butterball Nutria

1 12-lb. nutria, skinned and gutted as turkey
1 cup salad oil
1 bottle Russian dressing (with honey)
Salt and pepper to taste
4 lemons, sliced
1 12x12" pine board, sawdust free

Preheat oven to 350 degrees. Drill 30 ³⁄₁₆" holes in pine board, removing all sawdust. Attach nutria to pine board with 4 16" aluminum nails. Mix salad oil, Russian dressing, salt, and pepper. Pour into large baking pan and add sliced lemons. Add nutria, board-side up. Bake at 350 degrees for 60 minutes, basting board every 10 minutes or so. This allows the sauce to slowly drip through the holes, basting the nutria and keeping the board from drying out. Remove pan from oven. Detach board from nutria and place board on platter. Throw away the nutria and enjoy your pine board!

Recipe from *Oil and Gastronomy Cookbook*.

Foret's Fine French Foods

When that well-known and much-loved Creole chef Mrs. Aline Foret of Galliano put together her own cookbook in 1975, calling it *Foret's Fine French Foods,* it was a chance for everybody who had salivated over the dishes served in her hospitable dining room or kitchen to try to duplicate them at home. Not that anybody could ever quite match her fine French flair, but having the recipes was a start, and Mrs. Aline tried to make it easy by giving simple instructions for the most basic but necessary techniques, such as how to properly make a roux, the basis for many of her finest dishes.

She tested each recipe at least 3 times, sharing the results with friends and neighbors, and she says with a twinkle in her eye that one of her neighbors was outdone when the cookbook was finished. Not that the sharing of fine food ever stopped; Mrs. Aline loves to cook, and even strangers introduced for the first time are blessed with lovingly bestowed tins full of her homemade fudge and other sweets. She says she was never really taught to cook, it just came naturally, and for many years she served as a hospital dietitian, delighting patients and doctors alike with her culinary creations.

Creole cooking, Mrs. Aline explains, is plain and simple cooking, simmered on low heat to blend seasonings with the food, and always relying on onions, shallots, celery, garlic, and parsley. She recalls using the leaves of wild celery along with onions and garlic as a child; the bell pepper's popularity came later. These plentiful and standard seasonings must never overpower the food. Mrs. Aline's nephew Terry St. Cyr explains that traveling from the bayou toward Acadiana, from Creole to Cajun cooking, the cayenne is applied with a heavier hand as one travels west. "It has to burn your lips!" he jokes about Cajun cooking, and Mrs. Aline

agrees that Creole cooking, with its blending of African, German, and French influences, does not use an excessive amount of spices, just enough to enhance the natural flavor rather than overwhelm it.

A good cook, Mrs. Aline insists, must take pride in her achievement, devoting time, effort, and talent to her family's happiness, and a good husband, she insists just as strongly, should never fail to compliment the cook. "I know how to make a man happy," the 91 year old says with a wink. Nephew Terry agrees, recalling how she would lovingly peel tiny shrimp and arrange them just so around the sauce for her husband Gillis's shrimp cocktail. "No

one had any money," Mrs. Aline recalls of the old days, "but we lived good; my husband drank St. Julian wine."

Her mother died when Mrs. Aline was 3 years old, and her father never remarried. "He said a man had only one time to love in his lifetime. He was wrong; I think you can love more than once." Still full of life and good humor in her 90s, still an avid fisherman and gardener, Mrs. Aline recounts the story of a long, happy marriage beginning in 1935. After her husband's death, she spent many more years with a gentleman friend she jokingly calls her "playmate." At age 79, doing the Cajun Two-Step with her 88-year-old playmate, she won the dance contest at the Abbeville Omelet Festival, and she doesn't mind telling you, "I've done my share of dancing and gadding about!"

The absolute personification of joie de vivre, that enviable ability to relish life with gusto, Mrs. Aline has lived in various locations along the bayou and near New Orleans, also spending time along the coast to enjoy the fresh seafood and cooling sea breezes. In the 1930s she remembers renting a cabin at Grand Isle for $1 a day. In the '40s the family built a small 30x30' cabin with no indoor plumbing and no air conditioning, cows running around outside, and water for showers heated by the sun in a 55-gallon drum. This camp was destroyed along with all but 3 homes in the neighborhood by Hurricane Betsy in 1965. A later camp was broken off its pilings in a storm and blown several blocks away then sold for $1; it has now been resurrected as the slightly cockeyed Grand Isle base ("solid, yes; square, no!") for Terry St. Cyr, Mrs. Aline's nephew, who is one of the premier fishermen of the area, winner of the Grand Isle Tarpon Rodeo, Speckled Trout Rodeo, Golden Meadow Rodeo, Louisiana Sportsman's Calcutta, and the Hercules Rodeo, during which he hauled in the top-prize stringer of 5 speckled trout weighing 37.13 pounds. Terry has a camp full of trophies, but his most prized possession is his Aunt Aline's cookbook.

Mrs. Aline calls a roux the marriage of oil and flour and says the ingredients must be blended with the same loving care as any good marriage. Her instructions are clear: heat oil until hot but not smoking, remove pot from heat, add flour slowly and stir well, place pot on low heat and stir constantly until desired color. The copper of a new penny is a good color to strive for in a roux, or just a little darker.

Here are some of the recipes from Mrs. Aline Foret's fine French cookbook. Notice that her dishes are not only prepared with great care but are presented with just as much attention to detail, with special garnishes carefully chosen to set off each particular food and appeal to the eye as well as the palate. Mrs. Aline Foret has not forgotten how to please a man. As she says, "We can't all be stars, but we can twinkle!" And boy, does she twinkle!

Crabmeat Omelet

½ cup chopped shallots
½ ¼-lb. block butter
1 cup crabmeat
6 eggs
2 tbsp. milk
Salt to taste
White pepper to taste
1 tbsp. chopped parsley

Sauté shallots in butter. Add crabmeat; fold over to mix shallots with crabmeat. Beat eggs; add milk, salt, and pepper. Pour over crabmeat. Cook on low until eggs are set. Garnish with chopped parsley. Serves 4.
Recipe from Aline Foret.

Fried Soft-Shell Crabs

4 large soft-shell crabs
1 cup milk
2 eggs
2 tsp. yellow mustard
1 tbsp. Worcestershire sauce
Salt to taste
Cayenne pepper to taste
2 cups flour
Oil for frying
Cherry tomatoes

Soak crabs in milk for 30 minutes. Drain crabs and set aside. Beat eggs into milk, then add mustard, Worcestershire sauce, salt, and cayenne pepper. Spread flour on wax paper, coat each crab with flour, dip in egg, then coat with flour again. Deep-fry. Slit cherry tomatoes and place a sprig of parsley into tomato. Use as garnish. Serve with tartar sauce. Serves 4.
Recipe from Aline Foret.

Crabmeat Louis

Sauce

1 cup pure mayonnaise
½ cup chili sauce
1½ tsp. grated onion
1 tsp. horseradish
1 tsp. lemon juice
½ tsp. dried tarragon leaves
Salt to taste
Tabasco to taste

1 lb. lump crabmeat
4 large lettuce leaves
4 hard-boiled eggs, quartered
4 tomatoes, quartered

Mix sauce ingredients and chill overnight. Place ¼ crabmeat on each lettuce leaf. Pour sauce over crabmeat. Garnish with eggs and tomatoes. Serve with crackers. Serves 4.
Recipe from Aline Foret.

Trout Aline

4 fillets of trout
Salt to taste
Cayenne pepper to taste
4 tsp. butter
1 3-oz. pkg. cream cheese
2 egg yolks
2 tbsp. lemon juice
1 tsp. grated lemon rind
1 tsp. Creole mustard
2 tbsp. chives, chopped
Salt and pepper to taste
¼ tsp. Louisiana hot sauce
Seasoned breadcrumbs to top
Spiced peaches to garnish

Season trout well with salt and cayenne pepper; place on oiled steak plates and dot with butter. Cover with foil and bake at 300 degrees for 25 minutes. In double boiler on very low heat, melt cream cheese. Add one egg yolk at a time, beating briskly with wooden spoon after each addition. Add lemon juice, rind, mustard, chives, salt, pepper, and hot sauce. Place ¼ of sauce on each fillet, sprinkle with seasoned breadcrumbs, and dot with butter. Bake at 300 degrees until brown. Garnish with spiced peach fans. Serve with garlic bread. Serves 4.
Recipe from Aline Foret.

Bouillabaisse

2 large ripe tomatoes
1 cup chopped onions
1 cup diced celery
1 cup chopped shallots
3 cloves garlic, chopped
1 tbsp. parsley
2 tbsp. shallot tops
2 tbsp. chow-chow
1 bay leaf
1 tbsp. Worcestershire sauce
½ cup imported olive oil
1 cup sauterne wine
2 pt. small oysters, drained; reserve liquid
2 cups fish broth
4 pieces of fish (redfish, cobia, or red snapper)
Salt to taste
Cayenne pepper to taste
1 cup small shrimp, peeled
6 raw crabs, broken in halves
3 rock lobsters, shell on, cut in half
Stuffed olives for garnish

Slice tomatoes; divide tomatoes and seasonings through shallot tops into 3 equal parts. Mix chow-chow, bay leaf, Worcestershire sauce, olive oil, wine, oyster liquid, and fish broth; divide into 3 equal parts. Season fish with salt and pepper, then combine with all other seafood and divide into 2 parts. In heavy pot place a layer of seasoning, then a layer of seafood. Over this pour ⅓ of liquid. Repeat. You should have 3 layers of seasoning and 2 of seafood. Bring to a boil, cover well, and simmer on lowest heat. Cook 1 hour. Serve as you would soup. Garnish with slices of stuffed olives. Serve with French bread. Serves 4.
Recipe from Aline Foret.

Flounder Mornay à la Creole

White Sauce

¼ cup butter
2 tbsp. flour
1 cup scalded milk
Season to taste

2 flounder
Salt to taste
Cayenne pepper to taste
2 tsp. butter
1 tbsp. butter
2 tbsp. sliced shallots
2 tbsp. sliced mushrooms
1 tsp. yellow mustard
1 tsp. Worcestershire sauce
½ cup thick white sauce
3 tbsp. grated Swiss cheese
Salt and pepper to taste
Tabasco to taste
6 shrimp, boiled
2 slices bacon, fried crisp
Radish roses to garnish
Parsley to garnish

Melt butter in heavy saucepan, blend in flour, and cook on low heat. Stir constantly until smooth. Remove from heat and stir in scalded milk a little at a time. Season to taste and cook on low heat until bubbly.

Season flounder with salt and pepper and dot with butter. Place each fish on buttered steak plate, place foil over plate, and bake at 350 degrees for 25 minutes. Sauté sliced shallots and mushrooms in butter. Add mustard, Worcestershire sauce, white sauce, Swiss cheese, salt, pepper, and Tabasco sauce. Simmer until cheese melts. To serve, place one strip of bacon and 3 shrimp on each fish and top with sauce. Place in oven to heat. Garnish with radish roses and sprigs of parsley. Serves 2.
Recipe from Aline Foret.

Shrimp Étouffée

1 tsp. flour
2 tbsp. oil
2 cups chopped onions
1 cup chopped shallots
½ cup chopped celery
2 cloves garlic, chopped
2 tbsp. butter
2 cups small shrimp, peeled
¼ cup chopped parsley
¼ cup shallot tops
Salt to taste
Cayenne pepper to taste
2 tbsp. water
Black olives for garnish
Tomato wedges for garnish

Make roux using flour and oil. Add onions, shallots, celery, and garlic. Cook on very low heat in well-covered pot for about 40 minutes. Stir often. Add butter, shrimp, chopped parsley, shallot tops, salt, pepper, and water. Cover. Simmer on low heat for 20 minutes. Set aside to flavor for 20 minutes. Garnish with black olives and tomato wedges. Serve on rice. Serves 4.
Recipe from Aline Foret.

Eggplant Stuffed with Shrimp and Crabmeat

2 eggplants
½ cup chopped onions
¼ cup chopped celery
¼ ¼-lb. block butter
½ cup ground shrimp
¼ cup chopped shallots
3 cloves garlic, chopped
¼ bell pepper, diced
1 slice white bread
1 tbsp. chopped shallot tops
1 tsp. parsley
½ cup crabmeat
Breadcrumbs to top
Romano cheese, grated to top
Curly parsley to garnish
Stuffed olives to garnish

Cut eggplants in half and boil until tender. Scoop out eggplant meat and drain. Sauté chopped onions and celery in butter. Add eggplant meat and cook on medium heat for 10 minutes. Stir often. Add ground shrimp, chopped shallots, garlic, and bell pepper. Cook for 20 minutes. Soak bread slice, squeeze out excess water, add to eggplant dressing, and stir well. Add chopped shallot tops, parsley, and crabmeat; cook for 5 minutes. Fill eggplant shells and sprinkle with breadcrumbs and cheese. Bake at 325 degrees until browned. Garnish with curly parsley and stuffed olives. Do not cook in iron pot. Serves 4.
Recipe from Aline Foret.

Oysters: The Louisiana Coast's
Fabulous Fresh Seafood Harvests

Louisiana's oyster industry generates nearly $286 million a year and creates thousands of jobs. The state produces well over a third of the country's oyster harvest, some 13 million pounds, according to the state Department of Wildlife and Fisheries.

Oysters are cultivated in beds planted in waters leased from the state. Louisiana leases nearly 400,000 acres of state water bottoms through more than 8,000 private leases and manages 1.6 million acres in public oyster grounds. Thousands more acres are used as seed beds, nurseries for oysters that will be transplanted to private reefs. The oysters farmed on a commercial scale are planted in September, allowed to grow fat and salty, then harvested in early spring after the oysterman has spent the winter working the public beds. These oyster grounds are carefully monitored by the Office of Public Health for bacterial pollution to make sure the waters where oysters are grown remain safe so that Louisiana oysters can be eaten raw without hesitation.

The oyster industry recently has been conflicting with the state's fight to prevent coastal erosion. The industry seeks to strike the delicate balance required so as not to negatively impact either program. It is a hard balance to maintain, and part of it has been fought out in courts of law because wetlands erosion and subsidence have rendered historically productive areas of little significant oystering value. Oysters are killed by too much fresh water, though conversely too much saltwater attracts

predators like black drumfish or the oyster drill that eat the oysters in their shells. Freshwater diversion, an integral part of coastal restoration, can have a negative impact on the viability of the oyster industry, and so can the mountains of sediment dumped during diversion project construction, because oysters require a hard bottom to grow.

Besides the impact of man-made projects, oystering can be impacted heavily by hurricanes. Hurricane Ivan in 2004 caused tremendous damage due to saltwater and sediment stirred up by the heavy winds and waves, killing an estimated 263,000 sacks of Louisiana oysters worth more than $6 million (average price per sack generally runs around $14, though some years they approach $20 or $25 at the dock and nearly twice that retail). The hurricane's pounding waves tore some oysters from their beds, depositing silt and salty water that smothered others. Seed oysters destined for future years' harvests suffered the worst damage, but the state obtained federal grant money to fund some restoration efforts, mostly laying down new oyster beds that would be open to public harvest in season. In 2005, Hurricanes Katrina and Rita had a similarly devastating effect, but the industry always proves resilient.

While oysters in beds along the Chesapeake Bay or Long Island can take up to 4 years to mature to market size of 3 inches in length, Louisiana's warm waters in brackish estuaries encourage much more rapid growth to full maturity in half the time. As waters warm about the oyster reef in the springtime, eggs and sperm are released to join together in the surrounding waters, forming a larva that can swim freely for a few weeks, until the weight of its growing shell pulls it to the bottom. There the oyster remains, cemented to other oysters or shells, pumping water in and out.

Now the oyster luggers have mechanical dredges, heavy metal baskets that drag the bottom to scrape up the oysters as they methodically circle up and down the bay or bayou, but the harvest used to be done utilizing rakelike hand tongs with long wooden handles, the baskets of oysters hauled onto the deck manually. The men who hoisted the heavy sacks of oysters onto boat decks and then transport trucks, often Indians who were referred to in rather derogatory fashion as "Sabines," were always readily recognizable by the bulging muscles in their arms.

Today the luggers have round-bottomed hulls, flat canvas roofing over the foredecks, and gunwales built up amidships with a latticework of boards to keep the oyster sacks from falling overboard. The dredges with their nets are hauled up by chains and pulleys to dump their load of oysters onto the deck, where they are culled and separated.

Always popular with Louisianians, oysters traditionally have been especially prized during holidays like Christmas. Even in plantation country upriver from the coast, local merchants would order sacks of oysters shipped straight from the gulf as gifts for prominent customers and the big sugarcane or cotton planters who patronized their stores. The polished mahogany plantation dining tables groaned with special holiday feasts including oyster stew, oyster cornbread dressing, oysters Rockefeller, and fried or raw oysters. Even today, demand for oysters jumps at Thanksgiving, Christmas, and New Year's.

Some of the following recipes are provided by 91-year-old Creole chef Mrs. Aline Foret, while others come from the Web site of the Louisiana Seafood Promotion and Marketing Board, www.louisianaseafood.com, always an excellent source for information.

Creole Oyster Soup

2 tbsp. oil
2 tbsp. flour
⅓ cup chopped onions
⅓ cup chopped shallots
⅓ cup diced celery
2 cloves garlic, chopped
2 cups small oysters, drained
2 cups oyster liquid
1 tbsp. chopped shallot tops
1 tbsp. parsley
Salt to taste
Cayenne pepper to taste
Soup vermicelli (1 curl)
Lemon wedges for garnish

Make roux using oil and flour. Add chopped onions, shallots, celery, and garlic. Cook on low heat in uncovered pot until oil separates. Stir often. Add 1 cup oysters. Cook on high heat for 7-10 minutes. Contents will stick slightly to bottom of pot. Add oyster liquid, shallot tops, and parsley. Simmer on low heat for 30 minutes. Add remaining oysters, salt, and pepper. When oysters are plump, add vermicelli and simmer for 5 minutes. Set aside to flavor in covered pot for 20 minutes. Garnish with lemon wedges. Serve with crackers. Serves 4.
Recipe from Aline Foret.

Oyster Rice Dressing

½ cup chopped onions
½ cup chopped celery
½ cup chopped shallots
3 cloves garlic, chopped
4 tbsp. butter
1 pt. oysters, chopped and drained
¼ cup celery leaves
¼ cup shallot tops
2 tbsp. parsley
Salt to taste
Cayenne pepper to taste
2 cups cooked rice

Sauté chopped onions, celery, shallots, and garlic in butter. Add chopped oysters. Cook over medium-low heat for 3 minutes. Add chopped celery leaves, shallot tops, parsley, salt, cayenne pepper, and rice. Stir once gently with fork. Cover, place on low heat, and cook for 20 minutes. Serves 4.
Recipe from Aline Foret.

Oysters Supreme

½ cup chopped shallots
2 cloves garlic, chopped
½ cup chopped celery
2 tbsp. chopped shallot tops
1 tbsp. parsley
½ cup butter
1½ cups crushed plain soda crackers
1 pt. oysters, chopped; reserve liquid
¼ tsp. Tabasco sauce
Salt to taste
1 tbsp. Worcestershire sauce
Grated Romano cheese to top
Lemon wedges
Mint leaves

Sauté chopped shallots, garlic, celery, shallot tops, and parsley in butter. Add crushed crackers, chopped oysters, Tabasco, salt, Worcestershire sauce, and oyster liquid. Make this mixture very moist. Place in well-greased pan and top with cheese. Bake at 300 degrees until brown. Garnish with lemon wedges tipped in crushed mint leaves. Serves 4.
Recipe from Aline Foret.

Creole Oysters Rockefeller

10 oz. frozen spinach
½ ¼-lb. block butter
⅓ cup chopped onions
⅓ cup chopped shallots
⅓ cup chopped shallot tops
3 large cloves garlic, chopped
1 tbsp. capers
2 filets of anchovies
Salt to taste
Cayenne pepper to taste
24 fresh cocktail oysters
12 large oyster shells
½ tsp. butter
Breadcrumbs
Parmesan cheese
Lemon wedges
Cherry tomatoes

Place frozen spinach, butter, onions, shallots and tops, garlic, capers, and anchovies in well-covered heavy pot. Stir often. When spinach thaws, use egg spatula to chop spinach and seasoning. Each time you stir, chop also. Cook until dry, about 35 minutes. Season with salt and pepper to taste. Bring oysters to a boil in oyster liquid, just until oysters curl. Remove oysters and reduce liquid to about 4 tbsp. liquid. Place 2 oysters in each shell; add 1 tsp. oyster liquid, ½ tsp. butter, and place spinach on top. Sprinkle with breadcrumbs and top with grated cheese. Bake at 300 degrees until brown. Garnish with wedges of lemon and cherry tomato. Serves 2; 6 oysters each.
Recipe from Aline Foret.

Oysters Bienville

¼ cup butter or margarine
3 tbsp. flour
1 clove garlic
1 tbsp. onion juice
1 tbsp. Worcestershire sauce
¼ tsp. celery seed
¾ cup oyster liquid
1 2-oz. can mushrooms
18 medium Louisiana shrimp, boiled
1½ pt. medium Louisiana oysters
Parmesan cheese
Rock salt

To make sauce, melt butter and add flour, garlic, onion juice, Worcestershire sauce, celery seed, and liquid. Add mushrooms and shrimp. Cook until thickened. Put oysters in saucepan and simmer just until edges curl. Drain. Put oysters on cleaned oyster shells. Cover each with sauce mixture and sprinkle with cheese. Place on tray covered with rock salt. Broil for about 5 minutes or until bubbly. Serves 6.
Recipe from Chef Catherine Longman for Louisiana Seafood Promotion and Marketing Board.

Oysters in Oregano-Tasso Cream Sauce Over Linguine

4 oz. heavy cream
1 tbsp. minced tasso
½ tsp. oregano
12 fresh Louisiana oysters
Salt to taste
Freshly ground white pepper to taste
½ cups fresh linguine

In a medium skillet over high heat, place heavy cream, tasso, and oregano. Bring to a boil. Reduce heat and simmer until about half the amount of liquid remains. Add oysters and simmer about 1 minute or until edges of oysters just start to curl. Season with salt and freshly ground white pepper. Pour over linguine and toss together well. Serves 1.
Recipe from chef at the Westin Hotel, Canal Place, for Louisiana Seafood Promotion and Marketing Board.

Oysters and Artichoke Pan Roast

2 shallots, diced
¼ cup diced fennel
¼ cup diced leeks
Oil to sauté
24 Louisiana oysters
1 large tomato, diced
¼ cup white wine
4 artichoke hearts; reserve leaves for garnish
½ tsp. tarragon
½ tsp. basil
½ tsp. thyme
2 oz. butter
Salt to taste
Pepper to taste
Tabasco sauce to taste

In a 10-inch skillet, sauté shallots, fennel, and leeks in oil until clear. Add oysters and tomato and cook until edges of oysters are curled. Remove oysters and keep warm. Add wine and artichoke and reduce liquid by half. Add herbs and seasonings to taste and swirl in butter. Remove artichoke and place on plates. Return oysters to pan and heat through. Divide sauce evenly over artichokes and serve. Add Tabasco sauce to taste. Serves 4.
Recipe from Chef Kevin Visard for Louisiana Seafood Promotion and Marketing Board.

Shrimp Boats A'Coming

Louisiana's shrimp (*crevette*) season usually opens in late May in different zones in state waters up to 3 miles out, the opening date determined by marine biologists who test the size of the young shrimp; it closes the end of July, then reopens from August until December. Louisiana has 3 main kinds of shrimp: white shrimp, brown shrimp, and what are called seabobs (a corruption of the French *six barbes*). White shrimp make up the bulk of the fall catch and are said to be marketable size, large enough for the season to open, when the shrimp reach 100 to the pound. In the deep waters of the gulf, shrimping is open year-round, and it is the Gulf of Mexico's most profitable fishery, with annual sales of close to $500 million. Louisiana is the gulf's biggest shrimp producer. In the then-record year of 2000, Louisiana's shrimp fleet landed 47.3 million pounds of white shrimp (heads-off weight) between August and the end of the year. Louisiana, in fact, is the leading producer of all American shrimp, more than 120 million pounds a year.

Brown shrimp spawn during early winter and white shrimp during summer, with females laying up to a million eggs. The eggs hatch and the young shrimp go through a series of changes from planktonic to larval shapes, and while undergoing these

changes they somehow manage to migrate up to 50 miles through the gulf waters. They drift with the currents into the inland estuaries where they feed and grow for several months in the marshes, consuming rich nutrients and proteins unique to the Mississippi Delta until they are an inch or two long. Then they leave their brackish feeding grounds and migrate back out into the gulf, moving out of the marsh on tides controlled by the moon. During the migration, when the staging areas of the bays literally boil with young shrimp, shrimpers catch them in skimmers and butterfly-shaped trawl nets.

Shrimp populations grow in cycles, and not all years are good ones. Some shrimpers shrimp during the summer and crab in the winter to prevent a sole reliance on a good shrimp harvest. However, the traditional abundance of fresh seafood and Louisiana's rich culinary traditions have always ranked the state among top destinations for high-quality seafood harvest and consumption, and shrimping is an important part of the state's culture and heritage. In the Gulf of Mexico, there are around 3,000 shrimpers with federal licenses trawling from 3 to 200 miles offshore, and many more, about 14,000, with state licenses who shrimp closer to shore, within the 3-mile limit of state jurisdiction.

The seafood industry is now taxed and regulated stringently, with new requisite devices and rules designed to protect Kemp's ridley turtles, red snapper, and other threatened marine life; the TEDs, or turtle escape devices, also let shrimp escape and cut profits for the fishermen. Recently there have also been efforts to cap the number of commercial shrimpers allowed in federal waters. The annual shrimp harvests in the gulf in the last 50 years have ranged between 100 million pounds and 160 million pounds, but the drop in prices has led some to suggest that government-imposed limits on the fleet might help stabilize the industry according to the dictates of supply and demand, ensuring sustainability. Federal regulators have also considered the imposition of industry rules on gulf shrimping following the model of Alaskan fisheries, requirements for observers on boats to enforce laws regulating nets and bycatch, as well as electronic logbooks, vessel monitoring, and other measures seen as too costly and potentially devastating by an industry already threatened by cheap farm-raised foreign imports and rising operating costs like fuel.

According to the Southeastern Fisheries Association, the size of the offshore shrimp fleet could drop 40 percent in the next decade if the government imposes such regulations. Indeed, the state already has lost thousands of shrimpers since 2001; the shrimp catch in a single year dropped some 7 million pounds.

Still, the shrimp industry has come a long way since the days of Filipino and Chinese laborers boiling shrimp or fish in brine then drying them on huge raised cypress platforms in the broiling sunlight around Grand Isle and other locations. They could gut a fish with one jerk, flinging the innards to the huge white hogs waiting beneath the platforms to fight over the spoils, the odor strong enough to knock a grown man down. Camps on stilts around these raised drying platforms housed the workers, their families, and the fishermen as well as warehouses, general stores, even a post office at the largest ones like Manila Village. The women and children wore special shoes to "dance the shrimp," chanting and shuffling atop the drying shrimp to separate the shells. Then the shrimp were packed into barrels for export, which was ironic because many of the Chinese shrimp laborers had been smuggled into this country in barrels themselves.

Because of the extremely perishable nature of shrimp, in the early years the only preservation and processing methods were sun drying and canning. It would not be until improved refrigeration techniques emerged after World War II that Louisiana's serious commercial shrimping industry developed. Initially the shrimping was done with small cast nets, thrown by hand and weighted along the edges, then the larger haul seine, and finally the funnel-shaped otter trawl, pulled along the bottom behind a boat, that doubled the state's shrimp harvest the first year after it was introduced in 1919. Now many shrimpers use the paupiere, the picturesque butterfly net, usually in pairs, with a rectangular frame of tubing holding its mouth open and either pulled along through the waters or used in a fixed position where natural currents wash shrimp into the net.

Since 1972 Grand Isle has hosted the huge Wayne Estay Shrimp Company, located atop filled-in oyster beds and first leased in 1972 from John Blanchard. Tied up to the docks are dozens of shrimpers with tall booms that can be swung down

for trawling, some with 2 and some with 4 trawls. The butterfly nets are lowered by winches now, not pulled by hand, and the government limits the size and type of nets as well as the areas available for shrimping. Shrimping technique has progressed over the years from seining in the estuaries to trawling, from sailing luggers and then motorized Lafitte skiffs, and finally the big offshore shrimp boats equipped with modern technology, state-of-the-art communications equipment, and the refrigeration required to stay away from port for weeks at a time.

The Estay Shrimp Company provides rustic housing right by the docks for its shrimpers during season. The company deals in wholesale and retail shrimp and fish sales, the seafood fresh from the gulf. In peak season Estay may buy catches from 75-80 boats a day; average days, the company buys from 50 boats. Since the company is located on the unprotected north side of the island, the boats have to leave during hurricanes.

Shrimping has changed a good bit over the years, according to Wayne Estay's wife and sister, who run the office at the shrimp company. The industry is affected by the weather, changes in the coastline, government regulation, and foreign competition. The salvation of the industry, these

knowledgeable ladies feel, will come with remarketing, with educating the public on the benefits of fresh, wild American shrimp straight from the gulf and ocean waters.

Without increased appreciation for the unique and great taste of the natural, fresh product, domestic shrimp cannot compete with imported products coming from countries without government regulation, labor or wage limits, and other expenses that drive up the production cost in this country. Tariffs on foreign imports from Asia and South America, the ladies explain, work only until the taxed country begins sneaking shrimp through a third untaxed country to evade the government regulation. Shrimp accounts for about 25 percent of all seafood sold in this country, but some 85 percent of the shrimp Americans eat, an astounding number, comes from 6 countries: Brazil, Ecuador, India, Thailand, China, and Vietnam, all accused of dumping shrimp at unfairly low prices in the United States until the government imposed penalty tariffs on importers. Indeed, between 2000 and 2002, the value of the U.S. shrimp harvest was cut in half, from $1.25 billion to $560 million, because of competition from cheap canned and frozen imported shrimp.

And then came the devastating 2005 hurricanes, Katrina and Rita, whose combined impact on Louisiana's fisheries approached several billion dollars, considering losses to commercial and recreational fishing, shrimping, crabbing, and oystering, as well as damage to boats and infrastructure support like docks and icehouses, marinas and bait shops, and processing plants. Shrimp boats were sunk or damaged, and receding floodwaters left submerged debris to rip nets and sink additional boats. For an industry on the verge of collapse, even after record shrimp harvests in 2004, the storms were catastrophic, and for the Wayne Estay Shrimp Company, they swept away everything but the concrete slab.

Can a shrimper make a living now? Not really, the Estay ladies say, and many are forced to have alternate jobs on which to fall back. There's been a noticeable difference in the number of shrimpers, and Wayne Estay had predicted rather gloomily even before 2005's hurricanes that in ten years "nets in the water will be all over; it's a dying industry," although there are many dedicated die-hard shrimpers who will persevere.

The magazine ads, the ones with the shrimper in his rubber boots leaning rather despondently against the pier pilings with his shrimp boat in the background, tell the story:

> The majority of the SHRIMP you eat is imported pond-raised. Had we not been out catching the REAL THING we would've told you sooner." The ads go on to explain: "It's true. You aren't eating the shrimp we catch. No matter where you live, chances are your shrimp was raised in a pond and shipped overseas. Should you find that you'd much rather bite into authentic, wild-caught shrimp that's been naturally harvested from the Gulf and South Atlantic, be sure to ask for it. Learn more at www.wildamericanshrimp.com. Certified Wild American Shrimp: the shrimp you thought you were eating.

This is what the ladies at the Wayne Estay Shrimp Company are talking about when they say the future of the shrimping industry depends on the effectiveness of the remarketing campaign. Louisiana has always had a reputation for superior, fresh seafood of the highest quality, and consumers are mostly unaware that nearly three-fourths of the time what they are eating in local restaurants or even purchasing in local markets may be not as good or as fresh as it could or should be. The Wild

American Shrimp campaign, funded in part with federal grant monies, is designed to encourage chefs and diners, restaurateurs and entrepreneurs to be sure to ask for the fresh local shrimp, and it has received important support from famous names in Louisiana culinary circles.

The Blessing of the Fleet observances in coastal communities traditionally bring area priests to bayou or bayside to bless the shrimp boats and pray for safe and fruitful fishing; now they need to pray just as fervently for the success of the advertising and marketing campaign to reawaken the consumer to the blessings of fresh seafood just harvested in Louisiana's rich lakes and bayous, marshes, and gulf waters. Recent legislation mandates that the place of origin be listed on seafood packaging, so be sure to look for the Wild American Shrimp certification verifying that the seafood was caught in the wild and meets high standards of quality.

Some of the recipes listed here are from the Wild American Shrimp Web site, others from the Louisiana Seafood Promotion and Marketing Board's site at www.louisianaseafood.com, and still others are from Creole cook Aline Foret or Bubba and Beryl Eisworth, who are serious fishermen with a camp at Grand Isle, where they enjoy seafood fresh out of the gulf cooked in a variety of ways.

Beryl Eisworth says they cook often with boiled shrimp, and they peel the leftovers to add later to omelets, green salads, deviled eggs, or perhaps pasta cooked with cheddar sauce or garlic sauce. Life is casual on the island, and so are Beryl's recipes: just throw in whatever seems like a good idea, in whatever quantity and proportions you have, and somehow it all turns out to be delicious, especially with the soothing sound of waves echoing in your ears as brown pelicans fly by, the sun dips below the horizon and sets the gulf waters afire, a gentle breeze blows away the mosquitoes, and the air is perfumed with the complementary scents of sweet blooming oleander and spicy boiling shrimp.

Hot Shrimp Dip

1 cup shrimp, peeled
½ cup water
2 tbsp. chopped shallots
2 tbsp. chopped onions
2 tbsp. chopped celery
¼ cup butter
¼ cup flour
½ cup scalded milk
Salt to taste
Tabasco to taste

Boil shrimp in ½ cup water for 3 minutes. Drain shrimp but reserve broth. Grind shrimp and set aside. Sauté chopped shallots, onions, and celery in butter; add flour and blend well. Remove from heat. Add hot milk a little at a time, stirring constantly. Return to low heat, add shrimp broth, shrimp, salt, and Tabasco. Make this spicy. Bring to a simmer, stirring often. Cook 2 minutes. This may be used in cocktail patty shell.
Recipe from Aline Foret.

Shrimp Cornbread

2 eggs
1 15-oz. can cream-style corn
⅓ cup oil
¾ cup Cheddar cheese, shredded
1 box Jiffy cornbread mix
½ tsp. liquid crab boil
2 cups raw shrimp, diced
1 small onion, chopped
1 bell pepper, chopped
1 jalapeño pepper, chopped
1 4-oz. jar pimentos, drained
Tony Chachere's seasoning to taste

Mix eggs, corn, oil, and cheese. Stir in other ingredients. Bake in greased 9x12" pan at 350 degrees for 35-45 minutes until browned. Serves 6.

Sautéed Shrimp

1 large purple onion, diced
1 bell pepper, sliced
8 cloves garlic, sliced
8 stalks celery, chopped
½ cup olive oil
2-3 lb. shrimp
Salt to taste
Red pepper to taste
Basil to taste
Oregano to taste
Cumin to taste
Sugar to taste
Tony Chachere's seasoning
Paprika to taste
2 bunches shallots, chopped
1 bunch parsley, chopped

Lightly sauté onion, bell pepper, garlic, and celery in olive oil. Throw shrimp and vegetables in pot and bring to a boil. Stir repeatedly, adding lots of salt, red pepper, basil, oregano, and cumin. Wonderful! Also add sugar, Tony's, paprika, and other desired seasonings to taste. Reduce heat and steam until pink. Add shallots and parsley before serving. Good with heads on, but not everybody enjoys them that way. In Houma they use small, peeled shrimp served over rice and with a salad. On Grand Isle, they serve large, unpeeled shrimp with French bread to dip in the sauce, a baked potato, and a bib! In New Orleans they bake shrimp in butter and call it barbecue and serve with corn on the cob. Serves 6-8. Recipe from Beryl Eisworth.

Shrimp Logs

Leftover shrimp, cooked and chopped
1 pkg. cream cheese
1 tsp. lemon juice
Shallots, finely chopped
Dried parsley
Garlic, minced
Walnuts or pecans, chopped
Paprika

Form all ingredients into a log and roll in chopped walnuts or pecans. Sprinkle with paprika and chill overnight. Serves 6. Recipe from Beryl Eisworth.

Shrimp Boats

8 medium yellow squash
1 bell pepper
1 onion
Seasonings to taste
2 cups shrimp, peeled
2 cups French bread, toasted
1 stick margarine, melted
Cheddar cheese, grated

Boil yellow squash, cool, and slice lengthwise. Scoop out pulp. Throw pulp, bell pepper, onion, seasonings, shrimp, and French bread into a food processor. Add a stick of melted margarine and process. Stuff squash with mixture. Top with grated cheddar cheese and bake at 400 degrees until heated through and browned. Recipe from Beryl Eisworth.

Shrimp Stew

2 tbsp. oil
2 tbsp. flour
⅓ cup chopped onions
½ cup chopped shallots
⅓ cup chopped celery
2 cloves garlic, chopped
2 cups small shrimp, peeled
1 cup shrimp broth
2 tbsp. chopped shallot tops
1 tbsp. parsley
Salt to taste
Cayenne pepper to taste
2 eggs, boiled
Chives, chopped

Make roux using oil and flour. Add chopped onions, shallots, celery, and garlic. Cook over low heat until oil separates, stirring often. Add shrimp, broth, chopped shallot tops, parsley, salt, and pepper. Cover and simmer for 30 minutes. Set aside about 10 minutes to flavor. Garnish with egg wedges tipped in chopped chives. Serve over rice or on toast points. Serves 4.
Recipe from Aline Foret.

Shrimp Enchiladas

1½ lb. shrimp, cooked
1 10-oz. can cream of shrimp soup
1 10-oz. can cream of onion soup
1 cup picante sauce
1 8-oz. pkg. cream cheese, softened
½ cup sour cream
2 cups Monterey Jack cheese, shredded
1 bunch green onions, chopped
1 4.5-oz. can chopped green chilies
10 flour tortillas

Peel and chop shrimp. Combine undiluted soups and picante sauce over medium heat, stirring until heated through. Spoon 1 cup of this mixture into greased 13x9" casserole dish; reserve remaining mixture. Beat cream cheese and sour cream until smooth; stir in shrimp, 1 cup cheese, green onions, and chilies. Heat tortillas and spoon 4 tbsp. shrimp mixture down center of each. Roll tortillas and place seam side down in casserole dish. Pour remaining mixture over enchiladas and top with remaining 1 cup cheese. Bake at 350 for 30 minutes. Serves 6.

Louisiana Wild American Shrimp Piquante

3 tbsp. vegetable oil
1 medium onion, minced
3 ribs celery, minced
½ bell pepper, optional
3 garlic cloves, minced
1 14.5-oz. can crushed tomatoes, with juice
½ cup tomato sauce
1 lemon, cut in thin slices
1 lb. shrimp, peeled and deveined
Salt to taste
Pepper to taste
½ tsp. Tabasco sauce, optional
½ cup green onions, minced
½ cup fresh parsley, minced
Cooked rice, optional

Heat oil in 3-qt. saucepan. Sauté onion, celery, and bell pepper until very tender. Add garlic, crushed tomatoes with juice, and tomato sauce. Stir and bring this mixture to a gentle boil. Add lemon slices, stir, and cook for about 2 minutes. Add shrimp, salt and pepper, and Tabasco. Stir to coat well. Cook just until shrimp turn pink. Sprinkle with minced green onions and parsley. Serve over rice, if desired. Serves 4.

Microwave Shrimp Scampi

1 cup egg noodles
½ cup margarine
2 cloves garlic, pressed
2 tbsp. parsley, finely chopped
1 tsp. salt
½ tsp. pepper
1 tbsp. white wine
1 cup peeled Louisiana shrimp

Boil noodles until done. Melt margarine in ½-qt. microwavable dish for 1 minute on high. Add garlic, parsley, salt, pepper, wine, and shrimp. Microwave on high for 3 minutes and stir. Microwave on medium for 2 minutes. Let stand for 5 minutes. Serve over noodles. Serves 2.
Recipe from Chef Ashley Ridgedell for Louisiana Seafood Promotion and Marketing Board.

Shrimp-Stuffed Puffs

1 small onion
1 cup celery, chopped
½ cup chopped bell pepper
1 8-oz. can button mushrooms
6 tbsp. melted margarine
6 tbsp. flour
1¼ cups milk
3 tbsp. pimento, diced
3 tbsp. almonds, sliced
¼ tsp. salt
¼ tsp. pepper
6 drops Tabasco
¼ cup Parmesan cheese
¼ lb. Velveeta cheese
1 lb. medium Louisiana shrimp
Baked puff pastry shells

Sauté onion, celery, bell pepper, and mushrooms in margarine. Cook until wilted, but not brown. Slowly add flour, followed by milk, stirring to make a white sauce. Add remaining ingredients, except shrimp and pastry shells. Cook uncovered until cheese is melted. Add shrimp 5 minutes before serving. Serve over rice or in baked puff pastry shells. This may be made ahead, frozen, and reheated slowly on low heat. Serves 8.
Recipe from Chef Kyle Shirley for Louisiana Seafood Promotion and Marketing Board.

Grilled Shrimp with Mango and Melon Relish

Relish
1 ripe mango, julienne
½ cantaloupe, julienne
½ honeydew, julienne
1 cup seasoned rice vinegar
Juice of ½ lime
1¼ cup honey
1 tbsp. chopped cilantro
1 tbsp. chopped mint
¼ tsp. chili paste

Peel and cut in a fine julienne the mango and melons. Mix together the balance of ingredients. Refrigerate for 1 hour and drain.

Shrimp
2 lb. fresh Louisiana shrimp (10-15 count) with heads on
Salt to taste
Pepper to taste
2 tsp. Paul Prudhomme Shrimp Magic (or Creole seasoning)
Vegetable oil spray
Wooden skewers

Peel shrimp, leaving the heads attached, and split the back ¼ inch to remove the sand vein. Arrange in rows of 7-8 and double skewer. Season with salt, pepper, and Shrimp Magic on both sides. Spray with vegetable spray. Grill on a hot surface for about 2 minutes per side until just barely done. Be careful not to overcook. Serve with mango relish. Serves 4.
Recipe from Chef G. W. Fins for Louisiana Seafood Promotion and Marketing Board.

Andouille-Crusted Louisiana Shrimp

Egg Wash
3 eggs
⅓ gallon milk

Crust
2 oz. all-purpose flour
2 oz. breadcrumbs
2 oz. andouille sausage, cooked and ground
Salt to taste
Pepper to taste

Fresh Louisiana shrimp
2 large onions, sliced
3 bunches green onions, bias cut
6 shallots, shaved
Splash of cane vinegar
Salt to taste
Pepper to taste
Scuppernong preserves

In a large bowl, whisk together eggs and milk to create egg wash. Set aside. Combine all-purpose flour, breadcrumbs, andouille sausage, and salt and pepper. Set aside. Peel, devein, and clean shrimp thoroughly. Drag each shrimp through prepared egg wash. Shake excess egg wash off quickly, then drag immediately through crust mixture. Drop individual shrimp into deep fryer for approximately 1 minute each, or until cooked. Coat a medium sauté pan with olive oil and warm over medium heat. Grill sliced onions, green onions, shallots, cane vinegar, and salt and pepper until tender. Pile vegetables onto plate. Arrange crusted shrimp over grilled vegetables and spread reduced Scuppernong preserves around the perimeter of plate.
Recipe from Commander's Palace's Chef Tory McPhail's for Louisiana Seafood Promotion and Marketing Board.

Louisiana's Vanishing Coastline

The southern third of Louisiana seems to be mostly water related—bays and bayous, inlets and barrier islands, marshes and meandering rivers, estuaries, swamps, bogs and battures and beaches, you name it. Built up over thousands of years from the flooding and changing course of the Mississippi River, which brought in fresh floodwaters and sediment, which kept the coastal marshes healthy and growing, these coastal wetlands have been a boon to the state in providing abundant habitat for fish and shellfish and other wildlife valued for recreation as well as for a way of making a living, providing resting spots for migratory waterfowl, protecting inland areas from gulf storms, even filtering and cleansing the water. Louisiana's gulf coast is considered one of the world's most important and productive ecosystems.

But this is a fragile ecosystem, battered yearly by violent hurricanes and storm surges, interfered with by man's so-called improvements and progress. Louisiana is losing some 25-35 square miles of coastal wetlands every year, accounting over the last half-century for 80 percent of the coastal wetland losses of the entire country. Over the past 100 years, Louisiana has lost some 600,000 acres, roughly the size of a small state like Rhode Island or Delaware, and the loss contributes to flooding, pollution, and a lessening of important habitat area. In his compelling book *People of the Bayou: Cajun Life in Lost America,* author Christopher Hallowell calls this swampy-marshy delta country "a lost piece of America about to sink into the Gulf."

For major population centers like New Orleans and Houma, the terrifying prospect is exposure to

open water within the next 50 years if the Gulf of Mexico continues to advance inland at an unchecked rate. Even now, a direct hit on New Orleans by a major hurricane would be devastating, as was demonstrated in early 2005 when a group of students hung banners from French Quarter balconies to show how deep the water might be in that location as a result of a major storm: a shocking 18 feet! And if the water reached 18 feet in New Orleans, it would be a whole lot deeper in communities closer to the coast. In August 2005, of course, Hurricane Katrina and the ensuing levee breaks turned this hypothetical speculation into horrifying reality.

Louisiana's congressional delegation, lobbying for a larger share of oil and gas royalties generated offshore, insists a viable coastal restoration plan would cost at least $14 million, much of which should come from the federal treasury because the economic, energy, and environmental implications are nationwide.

In 1990 the Coastal Wetlands Planning, Protection and Restoration Act was enacted to provide some funding for coastal protection and restoration, and a variety of ongoing programs have been established to devise methods of holding and restoring Louisiana's vanishing coastal paradise. The scientists and marine biologists, the environmentalists and geologists, and even the politicians are all engaged, for this is after all the largest coastal wetlands area in North America and the 7th-largest wetlands delta in the world. But sometimes it seems that each group is suggesting a different approach toward solving this national crisis.

Certainly no one is more concerned about the issue or more dedicated to finding workable solutions than Louisiana's die-hard duck hunters, who know Louisiana's coastal wetlands like the backs of their hands, who recognize that these marshes have traditionally provided critical wintering areas for millions of ducks and geese using the Mississippi Flyway, and who have seen firsthand over the past several decades the unfolding catastrophe in this sportsman's paradise, stretching from the Sabine River in Texas to the Pearl River along the Louisiana-Mississippi border. Louisiana remains the number-one state in the nation in duck hunting, and the Mississippi Flyway is still the busiest of the migratory waterfowl routes, with Louisiana wetlands harboring the largest variety and number of ducks and geese anywhere in the country. But there is trouble in paradise.

A thorough examination of the trouble in Louisiana's endangered wetlands is provided in a beautiful book called *Vanishing Paradise: Duck Hunting in the Louisiana Marsh*, written by John R. Kemp and showcasing artist Julia Sims' amazing nature photographs. The book profiles some of Louisiana's 100,000 licensed waterfowl hunters and a number of duck-hunting clubs, both private

and commercial, informal or elaborate, some controlling tens of thousands of acres, and some so well established that several generations of the same families have been members over the last 75 years or so. The hunting lodges or clubhouses run the gamut from rustic to approaching luxurious; one—if stories can be believed—was once a rowdy brothel above a cockfighting ring and conveniently close to a roaring nightclub on the Texas highway in the heady days of the Spindle Top oil boom. Some hunting clubs have hosted celebrity guests; some welcome wives and daughters; many are close-knit groups of men enjoying relaxed male-only camaraderie and good cooking beneath humorous signs boasting "Martha Stewart doesn't live here."

The duck hunters are deadly serious, though, when it comes to the conservation of the coastal marshes. They are the ones out there in the duck blinds on those cold, frosty mornings, marveling as the marsh comes alive, the egrets and great long-legged herons fishing in the shallows, unblinking alligators cruising the still waters, snakes slithering silently across fallen logs as the sun rises to cast slivers of light through the morning mist. The hunter and his eager retriever strain to see or hear some sign heralding the approach of a flock of ducks or geese.

Today, some sections of the marshlands are suffering from saltwater intrusion caused by man-made navigation and petroleum exploration channels that changed the natural water-flow patterns. That intrusion negatively affects the aquatic vegetation ducks feed on and kills plants whose roots help to hold the land together, causing up to 30 square miles of coastal wetlands to erode from productive marsh to open water devoid of vegetation each year. Building up the levee systems along the major rivers of the state, especially along the Mississippi River after the devastating flood of 1927, prevented communities from being washed away but at the same time ended the natural spring flooding that over the centuries spread nutrient-rich sediments to nourish and maintain marshes in a natural building process. Hurricanes have devastated barrier islands that protected the coast, and other contributing factors include rising world sea levels, global warming, and natural subsidence.

To help combat the declining duck populations as well as the disappearing coastal marshes, both the state and federal government have preserved hundreds of thousands of acres as wildlife management areas and refuges with carefully maintained waterfowl habitat and sanctuaries. Conservation laws protect against the overkill that no doubt occurred in earlier centuries, when the ducks and geese were so plentiful that the skies were dark with migrating flocks, and commercial hunters sold boxcar-loads of dressed waterfowl iced down in barrels for shipment to restaurants around the country. As they sat on the water, the popular mallards and pintails were shot with heavy-gauge shotguns capable of killing a number of birds with a single shell, the lead pellets striking mostly in the head and back, the choice breast meat untouched.

Many duck hunting groups have joined other organizations in efforts to preserve and protect the coastal wetlands as well, planting vegetation to rebuild the marshes and barrier islands, imposing stricter bag limits, and improving habitats. The comprehensive Louisiana Coastal Wetlands Conservation and Restoration Task Force and the Wetlands Conservation and Restoration Authority have devised a cohesive strategic plan to work toward restoring and maintaining south Louisiana's wetlands: diverting sediment-rich waters from the Mississippi and Atchafalaya Rivers into marshes, constructing seasonal locks to stop saltwater intrusion, and restoring barrier islands and bottomland forests.

On average more than 3 million ducks winter in the state, and many of those end up in black iron pots simmering on stoves all over south Louisiana, for even when there is trouble in sportsman's paradise, the eating is still good. From the marshes come an abundance of wild duck as well as redfish from the shallow ponds, speckled trout from the canals, and shrimp and oysters and crabs, the bounty of the Louisiana bayous and coast. Nowhere are these prepared better than in the duck hunters' camps, which offer some of the best food in Louisiana and have provided early hands-on training for some of the state's most acclaimed chefs.

A few recipes are provided here, including one provided by Whitehall Plantation for *Vanishing Paradise*. For other duck recipes straight from the hunting camp, order *Vanishing Paradise* from Pelican Publishing; phone 800-843-1724 (online www.pelicanpub.com).

Whitehall Plantation's Roast Duck

3-5 frozen ducks
Salt
1-2 onions
2 bay leaves per duck
1 pt. cooking sherry
¼ cup cooking oil
¼ stick butter
1 cup water
2 2-oz. bottles onion juice
1 tbsp. chopped parsley
1 tbsp. sage
½ tsp. cayenne pepper
1 tsp. white pepper
1 pkg. Uncle Ben's Wild Rice (or more if needed)

Thaw ducks in cold water. Salt inside and out. Put ¼ onion and 2 bay leaves inside each duck. Place ducks, breast down, in a large roaster. Heat sherry, oil, butter, water, onion juice, parsley, sage, and both peppers to a boil and pour all of mixture over the ducks. Put the top on the roaster and cook at 350 degrees for 4-5 hours until ducks fall apart. Cut ducks in half and place back in juice to prevent drying. Serve ½ duck to each person with rice. May use juice over rice.

Wild Ducks

4 wild ducks
1 envelope Lipton onion soup mix
1 14-oz. can mushrooms
4 large squares heavy foil
½ cup red wine, sherry, or Cointreau
4 large carrots, cut into thirds

Skin ducks and remove all fat. Rinse. While still damp, roll each duck in dry soup mix. Place duck breast down on foil, surround with mushrooms, add a tablespoon or so of sherry or wine, and stick carrot pieces into duck cavity. Roll up edges of foil to seal tightly. Place foil packets on baking sheet in 300-degree oven and cook until tender, about 1½-2 hours for teal and 2½ hours for big ducks. Before unwrapping ducks, poke a hole in bottom of foil packet and drain gravy into gravy boat. Can dilute gravy with a little warmed red wine if too salty. Serves 4-8.
Recipe from Lucie Butler.

Grand Isle and Louisiana's Coastal Islands

Once there were 4 of them along this stretch of the Louisiana coast: Grand Isle, Grand Terre, Cheniere Caminada, Isle Derniere (or Last Island). Now there is essentially only one, Grand Isle, which has become the new "last" island. Louisiana's only inhabited and forested barrier island, 7½ miles long and a mile across at its widest, the new "last" island puts its faith in Le Bon Dieu and in its carefully cultivated trees that it will not repeat the fate of the original Isle Derniere.

Louisiana's gulf fringe is engaged in a never-ending struggle. Louisiana writer Harnett Kane, who loved and understood the area, as far back as the 1940s wrote that no other part of the coast was such a battlefield of elements all working for change, upbuilding, disintegrating by turn, wearing,

scouring, or depositing. He called lower Louisiana a place unable to make up its mind whether to be earth or water, and so belonging wholeheartedly to neither element, it instead blurred the distinction between the two. The Mississippi River shifts its route to the gulf and starts new deltas, dumping heavy soil during floods to build up land and provide footing for plant roots, then depositing pesticide run-off and pollution fatal to struggling sea life. The logging and canal cutting by man undermine the ability of the inland marshes and swamps to withstand saltwater surges. But of course it's the violent storms of summer, the dreaded hurricanes that rear up out of the Gulf of Mexico with unbridled fury, that wreak the most havoc.

Settled sporadically during the Spanish reign in the late 1700s by entrepreneurs with delusions of plantation grandeur, the islands proved less than hospitable to slave-tended crops of sugarcane and cotton due to the constant brine baths brought in by the sea breeze and the salty, sandy soil. When the early profiteers departed, others moved into southernmost Louisiana, men with less extravagant dreams. These were simple, down-to-earth fishermen and trappers, men who lived with their families in small, unpretentious cabins elevated on stilts safe from the floodwaters, and they took their living from the sea and the land—catching fish, shrimp, oysters, and crabs, trapping fur animals, eating well, and eking out a seasonal subsistence living.

And then into the melting pot were thrown 2 more influxes to influence the fate of these islands—the pirates and the pleasure-seekers. When the British captured many pirate lairs in the Caribbean in the early 1800s, the swarthy freebooters who were the scourge of mercantile shipping had to seek out new hideouts or give up preying on the rich booty of the Spanish Main, along which moved the newly mined gold and other wealth of the New World en route to the Old World. Louisiana's coastal waters had long provided safe

haven for various small-scale smuggling operations dealing in all manner of contraband, and Grand Terre, just east of Grand Isle in Barataria Bay, attracted the infamous Jean Lafitte.

Islanders to this day prefer to label the dashing Lafitte and his band as more socially acceptable "privateers," operating under legitimate letters of marque from tiny Cartagena in Colombia. In appreciation for aid in its rebellion against Spain, Cartagena licensed the pirate galleons to attack enemy Spanish vessels, a license liberally interpreted to include almost any promising vessel that came within reach. Unlike other cutthroats, the Lafittes generally allowed their captives to live, as the pirates were more interested in the fortunes to be made selling smuggled sea cargo and the "black ivory" of slaves, which Louisiana purchasers were only too happy to take off their hands at cut-rate tax-free prices.

Jean and his cross-eyed brother Pierre set up headquarters on Grand Terre, constructing a large storeroom, slave barracoon, and heavy fortifications, but base operations often extended to the other islands. The bay filled with strange ships both small and large, and the island population was swelled by reckless opportunists from many nations. They brought violence, bloody knife fights

GRAND ISLE, LA.

A Good Place to
Eat and Dance

SMITTY'S
CASINO
BAR & RESTAURANT

on land and quick, merciless deaths in shark-infested gulf waters. But they brought untold riches as well. The bays and bayous provided not only unfathomable labyrinths of escape routes no pursuer could possibly navigate, but also a direct passage into New Orleans, where much of the plunder was openly sold to eager buyers from booths in Pirate's Alley.

Even after the English tried to buy his help and an American fleet destroyed his Grand Terre fortifications, Jean Lafitte joined Andrew Jackson's rag-tag forces and provided much-heralded help to defeat the larger and better trained British force in the Battle of New Orleans. Pardoned and praised, some of the 1,000 or so pirates in Lafitte's band moved on, but some stayed, as no doubt many were locals.

Lafitte lieutenant Louis Chighizola came from Genoa and was called Nez Coupe. One version of the story says he got the name after losing at least part of his nose for love in a knife duel over a woman; another version told by a Rigaud descendent says his nose was snapped off with a bullwhip after he abused a female servant rented to him by slave-holding Jacques Rigaud, who happened by on his white horse as Chighizola was beating his slave. Chighizola, who owned a fruit stand in New Orleans' French Market, settled on Grand Isle, where his name lives on today. The descendants of

Jacques Rigaud from Bordeaux, one of the early land grant holders, remain on Grand Isle as well. Though they insist his connection with the band of pirates was more acquaintance than ally, one descendant says Rigaud indeed supplied Lafitte with fresh vegetables and fruit for his ships. The Lafitte lieutenant called the most bloodthirsty, Johnny Gambi, settled on Cheniere Caminada and raised a large family, and another pirate lieutenant went to New Orleans and became a popular politician.

After the pirates settled down to a modicum of respectability or moved on, to the islands came the pleasure-seekers. In the 19th century Isle Derniere was a popular seaside resort, the most fashionable watering place of wealthy aristocrats. It was crowded in season with fun-loving sun seekers and billed as "the Little Deauville of the South." Families, traveling by steamboat with enormous entourages of children and servants and trunks full of fashionable clothing, arrived to spend the entire season fishing and hunting, picnicking, yachting, bathing in the surf, dining on the day's catch still practically dripping with gulf waters, and dancing the night away.

The main hotel, the Trade Winds, was planned to be expansive and impressive, over 1,250 feet long, with 2 grand galleries over a raised basement, 3 central towers, a commodious dining room, and an

SEPT 5th 1932

elegant ballroom. The island also boasted smaller guest cottages and summer houses, bathhouses, and promenades.

It was without doubt a gay destination. Besides the recreational and social enticements, however, Isle Derniere had a more practical lure, for that dreadful scourge of Louisiana's hot and humid mosquito season, yellow fever, was thought to be less apt to spread so rapidly near salt water and sea breezes. Before Walter Reed established that the responsibility for the spread of the disease lay with the mosquito, yellow fever had killed more than 175,000 in crowded 19th-century New Orleans, spreading like wildfire to wipe out whole generations of families.

In August 1856 the social season on Isle Dernier was at its peak, when one day the bright sunshine and gentle surf gave way to ominous dark clouds and great breakers growing higher and higher. The wind intensified to a furious tempest and the rain poured violently, illuminated by brilliant streaks of lightning. The hotel guests, trapped upon a bare spit of land between 2 raging seas, bravely danced to the music in the ballroom until a great roar of wind and waves burst upon them. Families were swept away, frantic fathers losing their grip on small children, wives and mothers screaming as they were torn from their loved ones, all grabbing at floating tabletops or bits of flotsam to try to

remain afloat, battered and bashed by wave-pushed debris. The hotel cracked apart, whole sections falling into the raging waters.

As the sun rose the next morning, dazed survivors wandered about an island swept clean of vegetation; none of the 100 structures remained, and more than 200 people had been killed. Hands protruded grotesquely from beneath the sand on the beach, and bodies floated facedown in the waters, swept out to sea and then washed ashore again by the incoming tide. The hurricane of 1856 sounded the death knell for Isle Derniere.

For Cheniere Caminada, the killer storm would be the late-season fast-moving hurricane of 1893. This Isle of the Chitimacha, originally named for its early Indian inhabitants, was a cheniere that eventually took the name of the wealthy Spanish merchant Francisco Caminada, who acquired the property. By the late 1800s there were many small houses filled with families, many of them descended from Jean Lafitte's pirates. Life was good among their vineyards and orange groves, at least until the 1st of October 1893, when a hurricane smashed the sleeping cheniere, 125-mile-an-hour winds raging and waves reaching 20 and even 30 feet, then surging up the bayous to wipe out unwary residents inland. The death toll included more than half the population of 1,500, 750 lives lost, far more than the Isle Derniere tragedy. Of the

300 family houses on Cheniere Caminada, only 13 were left, and not a single boat was still seaworthy, devastating to a resident population in which more than 80 percent of the males were illiterate fishermen.

Besides the human toll, the hurricane also destroyed a good bit of Fort Livingston on Grand Terre, the brick fort the government had constructed to replace Jean Lafitte's fortifications guarding the entrance to Barataria Bay. Outer bastions were ripped off, and an entire wall crumbled into the gulf. Along LA Highway 1 may be seen the austere Cheniere Caminada Cemetery, with its historic marker commemorating the 1893 hurricane and its victims, many buried here in mass graves.

The lessons of these tragedies were not lost on the residents of Grand Isle, where the treasured trees and other tropical vegetation had firmer soil in which to put down roots. The trees in turn held the soil and provided windbreaks and shelter, not to mention all-important shade. The northern side of the island along Bayou Rigaud is lush with ferns, banana trees, palmettos, palms, and towering oaks, and even the beach side is brightened by immense, hardy oleander bushes covered throughout most of the year with colorful blooms. Though hard hit by hurricanes like the infamous Betsy, Camille, and Katrina that did so much damage all along the Gulf Coast, the determined little Grand Isle has prevailed. Its all-important trees help to hold it together, though they sometimes look as they did to 19th-century Louisiana writer Lafcadio Hearn, who described a group of Grand Isle oaks leaning away from the sea in terror, their stooping silhouettes suggestive of "fleeing women with streaming garments and windblown hair, bowing grievously and thrusting out arms desperately northward to save themselves from falling."

Though early settlers found life on Grand Isle to be less than rewarding and many of the early land grant holders departed, some remained, and there are still some houses left on Grand Isle that date from the 1800s, hidden among the trees on the forested side of the island, where many of the true islanders live. One historic home, built by the Naccari family in 1875, was used for worship for many years after the 1893 hurricane destroyed the area church. Others house descendants of the early Chighizola and Rigaud families. Another has a walkway of old brick salvaged when the home of

Nez Coupe was demolished, and yet another house was built in 1894 by the Hurricane Relief Fund and then floated to its present location in the storm of 1915.

After the early plantations failed, there were later experiments in farming diamondback terrapins in underwater pens for live shipment in barrels to eager restaurateurs or cultivating vegetables fertilized with shrimp shells and planted early enough in the growing season to beat to the market similar crops from other states. None of these early endeavors proved as profitable, or as enduring, as the 2 industries that sustain the island today: vacationing tourists and fishermen, both sportfishermen and those harvesting their catches for profit. Supplemented by oil-related businesses, the vacationers and sportfishermen sometimes swell Grand Isle's year-round population of less than 2,000 to 10 times that many, especially during such popular activities as the Grand Isle International Tarpon Rodeo or for holidays like the Fourth of July.

On Grand Isle, rental beach cottages raised on sturdy piers are capable of accommodating large families, and there are also motels and restaurants that cater to visitors. The Grand Isle Tourist Commission can provide complete information by telephone at 985-787-2997 or online at www.grand-isle.com. Grande Isle State Park has a visitors' center, a mile of beachfront, fishing pier, raised observation tower, and campgrounds. The Grand Isle Cemetery dates from the 1800s and contains interesting early graves, with some headstones inscribed in French. The gravestone of Nez Coupe's son, for example, reads, *"Ici repose la dépouille mortelle du vénérable Louis Chighizola, époux d'Anastasie Barthelemy, né le 18 Fev. 1820, décédé dans le sein de sa famille le 24 Mars 1893."* Island tradition has it that the bones of old Nez Coupe himself were reinterred within this same tomb when the old pirate cemetery was built over.

The Grand Isle Shipyard was established just after World War II to repair boats, fishing vessels, oil rigs, and ocean-going vessels and is one of the largest employers on this island in a state that has more shipbuilding establishments than any other. Another big employer on Grand Isle is Exxon-Mobil. For landlubbers, the island has nature preserves and hiking trails through the lush tropical vegetation. The Grand Isle Loop of America's

Wetland Birding Trail on the Louisiana Great Gulf Coast promises an overwhelming diversity of resident and migratory birds in a vast array of habitat areas, from bays and shoreline to salt marsh and meadows; each April the Grand Isle Migratory Bird Celebration includes field trips to see nesting brown pelicans and other birding opportunities. There's even a fabulous free Butterfly Dome on the grounds of the Grand Isle Port Commission, treating observers to a close-up appreciation of the stages of butterfly development amid a colorful array of flowering plants growing inside a greenhouse-cloth-covered geodesic dome.

The world has discovered what the islanders have known all along: there is unrivaled world-class fishing in the gulf waters and inland bays surrounding Grand Isle. The fishing runs the gamut from surf casting to pier and bridge fishing as well as inland and deepwater trolling. This is an island that has, not surprisingly, more boats than cars. Numerous marinas, bait shops, charter-boat services, and fishing guides make it easy for visitors to fish for a huge variety of fish, especially specks and reds inland or red snapper, king mackerel, tarpon, tuna, and marlin offshore. There are dozens of well-established fishing rodeos, and many a record has been set in Louisiana's coastal waters, including the 1,018½-pound blue marlin (record set in 1977), 310-pound broadbill swordfish (1980), 891-pound bluefin tuna (1981), and international record-setting 50¼-pound red snapper (1996).

The Gulf Restoration Network, which works to prevent additional damage to coastal wetlands and promote healthy fisheries, estimates Louisiana's fishing industries generate $800 million in commercial landings and $5.6 billion in recreational expenditures annually, a lot of that centered right around Grand Isle. This group and others keep a wary eye on proposals to develop natural gas terminals in the gulf and to increase aquaculture programs by rejuvenating idle offshore oil and gas platforms as fish farms.

Consumption of fish is more popular than ever now that the health benefits of omega-3 fatty acids found in many types of fish have been proven to help improve brain function and protect the body from certain diseases and disorders. Bubba and Beryl Eisworth have a camp on Grand Isle and have landed a number of trophy fish in various rodeos there. In 2006 Beryl became the first woman to win the Grand Isle Speckled Trout Rodeo, with husband Bubba coming in third. Some of their best recipes follow (you'll notice that they don't always cook the same dishes the same way).

Fish Dip

2 lb. redfish or snapper
Tony Chachere's seasoning
1 lb. cream cheese
¼-½ cup chopped onion
¼-½ cup chopped bell pepper
¼-½ cup chopped shallots
Parsley, chopped
2 cloves garlic, chopped
Dash of hot sauce

Season fish on both sides with Tony's seasoning. Bake fish on a cookie sheet at 350 degrees, cool, and flake. Add to cream cheese and mix together with a fork. Add chopped onion, bell pepper, shallots, parsley, garlic, hot sauce, and Tony's seasoning to taste. Refrigerate several hours so the flavors blend. Makes tons!
Recipe from Beryl Eisworth, adapted from her nephew Scott's recipe for catfish dip. Beryl says this is like tuna fish in that it can be spread on sandwiches as well as used for dip.

Grilled Redfish

Redfish
Tony Chachere's seasoning to taste
Lemon pepper to taste
Garlic to taste
Onion salt to taste
Italian dressing for marinating
Butter for basting
Lemon juice for basting

Season redfish (with the hide on) with seasonings to taste. Marinate 4-8 hours in Italian dressing with meat side down in refrigerator. Grill with hide down over medium-hot coals, using pecan chips. Season fish again and baste with butter and lemon juice as it cooks. Cook until opaque and fish flakes with a fork. Lift with large spatula, scooping the fish off the hide and leaving the "red" stuck to the hide. Place on a warm platter and squeeze lemons on top.
Recipe from Bubba Eisworth.

Redfish Court Bouillion

½-1 cup flour
½-1 cup bacon fat
2 cups chopped mixed vegetables (onions, celery, bell pepper, garlic)
1 8-oz. can tomato sauce
2 3-oz. cans tomato paste
4 lemons, halved
Redfish
White wine Worcestershire sauce
Tabasco sauce
Bay leaves
Tony Chachere's seasoning
Thyme
Oregano
Basil
Several pinches sugar
Water for thinning
Parsley
Shallots

Make a dark roux by browning equal amounts of flour and bacon fat. Add to roux 2 cups chopped vegetables (the Sam's Club chopped mix works well). Stir until well wilted. Add tomato sauce, tomato paste, and at least 4 lemons halved and squeezed. As this cooks slowly, add chunks of redfish (red part cut off) and gently stir. To this add white wine Worcestershire sauce, Tabasco, bay leaves, Tony's seasoning, thyme, oregano, basil, and several pinches of sugar. Cook this "most of the morning." When almost done, add water to make it the consistency of stew. Just before serving remove lemon peels and bay leaves, then add fresh parsley and shallots. Serve over rice. Serves 18-20.
Recipe from Beryl Eisworth.

Redfish Fettucine

1 cup chopped mixed vegetables (onions, celery, bell pepper, garlic)
1½ sticks butter
3 lb. redfish, cut into chunks
1 pt. Half and Half
Tony Chachere's seasoning to taste
Basil to taste
Rosemary to taste
Thyme to taste
Sugar to taste
Fettuccine
Parmesan

Sauté chopped vegetable mix in butter. Add redfish and slowly cook until flaked. Add cream and seasonings to taste. Bring to a boil. Reduce heat and cook 10-15 minutes. Serve over cooked fettuccine. Stir and add Parmesan. Cover and keep warm until served. Serves 6-8.
Recipe from Beryl Eisworth.

Sautéed Trout

Trout fillets (allow at least 1 per person)
Evaporated milk
Seasoned flour
Butter
Lemons

Soak fillets in milk at least 30 minutes. Drain. Flour with seasoned flour and place on a hot skillet sprayed with Pam. Brown in butter. Flip over once. Serve immediately with lemons squeezed on top. Also good with lemon fish or snapper.
Recipe from Bubba Eisworth.

Sautéed Trout

Trout fillets
Evaporated milk
Egg
Seasoned flour
Butter
Olive oil or Canola oil
Heavy cream
White wine
Mushrooms
Shallots, chopped
Garlic, chopped
Bell pepper, chopped
Shrimp, peeled
1 cup chopped walnuts

Soak fillets in equal parts milk and water mixed with egg for at least 30 minutes. Drain. Lightly flour with seasoned flour. Brown on both sides in equal parts butter and oil. Add heavy cream and white wine to skillet. "Then," Beryl says, "I go nuts and add whatever: mushrooms, shallots, garlic, bell pepper, small peeled shrimp, and seasonings." Cover and simmer 1-2 minutes. An alternative preparation browns the fillets in butter, removes them to a hot platter, and tops them with a cup of chopped walnuts seared in left-over butter in the skillet; pour over fillets and serve at once.
Recipe from Beryl Eisworth.

Baked Fillets

Fish fillets
Rotel tomatoes, drained
4 shallots, sliced
4 tbsp. breadcrumbs
4 tsp. Parmesan
4 tsp. butter, melted
1 tsp. grated lemon peel
2 tsp. lemon juice
2 tsp. hot sauce

Bake fillets 15 minutes at 450 degrees. Top with mixture of other ingredients and return to oven, cooking until fish is opaque and flakes with a fork. Beryl adapted this from a Weight Watchers recipe, and says its simplicity is welcome after a few days of Grand Isle fried food. Serves 1-2 fillets per person.
Recipe from Beryl Eisworth.

Old Grand Isle

In 1888, when he wrote *Chita,* the lovely little novella loosely based on the hurricane that had wiped out the seaside resort on Isle Derniere, writer Lafacadio Hearn in his inimitable style painted a poetic picture of the constant state of flux along Louisiana's coastline:

> Forever the yellow Mississippi strives to build; forever the sea struggles to destroy;—and amid their eternal strife the islands and the promontories change shape, more slowly, but not less fantastically, than the clouds of heaven.

Hearn was an astute observer, not just of nature but of man, and he recognized this erosion and regeneration not only of lands but of cultures as well.

And yet, the more things change, the more they stay the same. Grand Isle has taken the place of the lost Isle Derniere as a coastal resort, and the tourists sweep in like a tsunami, swelling the population of this tiny barrier island with each summer season, filling the rental cabins and raised camps, dotting the beaches with umbrellas and lounge chairs, crowding the little restaurants and bars. They may never even notice that there is another, totally different level of living on the island, that of the full-time long-term residents. To hear about this other lifestyle, just get a couple of the natives together, like crabber Raleigh Lasseigne and his good buddy Clovis Aubin Rigaud, and the stories flow, flavored with French accents and colorful details.

Raleigh Lasseigne was born just up Bayou Lafourche in Galliano; his father was a shrimper and oysterman. Raleigh moved to Grand Isle when he was 15, in the late '50s. Now, when he's not holding court in the cool of the evening in his

porch swing while his wife cooks up the day's catch, he crabs in the bay in summer and harvests oysters from the bay in winter, selling them in a small stand by his simple home on the island. Aubin Rigaud's ancestors were some of Grand Isle's earliest pioneers and held some of the first land grants from the Spanish government. Both men remember plenty of hard times on the island, and yet you can tell they would never live anywhere else.

Aubin Rigaud, Raleigh Lasseigne, and the other island youngsters worked hard, even as small children. Says Rigaud, "You didn't have to rock me to sleep at night." He chopped driftwood hauled by horse cart from the beach, sometimes selling it for $1 a cartload. The collecting was far from risk free, since poisonous snakes were known to ride the logs over from the mainland, and his grandfather warned that if he saw the horse put his ears up, he'd better look out for a snake. Lasseigne also remembers tonging oysters for $1 a day back when a full, heavy sack of oysters brought $2. Rigaud packed cucumbers for 50 cents a day, $3 a week, and gave it all to his mother; she'd give back him a quarter for himself, but then he could go to the movies for 16 cents.

Rigaud's childhood nickname poked fun at his patched clothes; the few new clothes the family had were ordered from Montgomery Ward. He got his first pair of tennis shoes when he was about 11 or 12 and needed to dress up for the cardinal's much-anticipated visit to the island for confirmation and communion at the Catholic church. And Raleigh Lasseigne's wife, Kay, only had one new dress in her entire life until she married.

Lasseigne's mother never learned English; Rigaud, who went to the one-room school on Grand Isle that housed the entire elementary group, says he didn't know a word of English until he got to school. He jokes that he could walk on paper all the way to the bridge, miles away, if he were to lay down all the punish work he had been forced to write, all the sheets filled with "I will never talk French."

Aubin Rigaud's great-grandmother was blind, and as a child one of his jobs was to lead her everywhere, even to the outhouse. His grandmother was a midwife, and he escorted her on jobs "rain, shine, or snow." She charged $10, and Rigaud says more than half of her patients could not pay, but she helped them nevertheless. He was born the year they built the wooden bridge to Grand Isle, 1932. Before that, the island was accessible only by water, and tourists would arrive on the freight boat. When bridge construction began, Rigaud's family owned a horse and cart and earned 15 cents a week transporting 3 workers; labor on the bridge was mostly by hand, and the pay was 85 cents a day.

Indians would sometimes come to the island in

pirogues with prime furs to trade. For the Indians' mink, otter, and muskrat skins the Grand Isle residents traded cows, and Rigaud's grandfather generally traded to his advantage. A cow valued at $1.50 brought furs he could sell for many times that amount. There were loose cattle and horses ranging all over the island until the stock laws of 1959, when cattle were sold for $5 a head. Islanders didn't eat beef because there was no way to preserve it without electricity. They mostly raised hogs, and when they butchered, they used every portion of the pig but the hoof.

Fresh water was highly valued and was caught in cisterns. "You got a quart per person to bathe in," Rigaud remembers, "a cat bath, so I swam in the bay in the evening and came in with my hair stiff like barbwire from the salt in it. But grandpa's horse drank 10 or 12 gallons of water a day; the horse worked, and he had priority."

Before the war, the big agricultural crop on the island was cucumbers, planted the second day of February to beat Florida crops to market; sometimes it worked and sometimes it didn't. When the weather didn't cooperate, sending a "nor'wester" with frigid temperatures and high winds—there were no weather reports to warn the farmers ahead of time—the whole family, wives and husbands, grandparents and children, would race through the fields frantically covering the fragile plants with wooden pyramids for protection. During good years some 250 crates of cucumbers could be shipped out in a single day, bringing in serious money for that time, especially when Grand Isle "cukes" hit the French Market first. Rigaud's father and grandfather were the only individuals on the island who plowed, and they were in great demand. The cucumber boom petered out during the war because there was no transportation for the crop.

Although Aubin Rigaud's ancestors had owned most of Grand Isle at one time, a good bit of the land was lost for nonpayment of taxes during the tough years. Surrounded as they were by the bounty of the sea, the folks of his grandparents' generation lived mostly on seafood, and so did some of the succeeding generations. Both Lasseigne and Rigaud recall when an LSU expert had to be summoned to provide dietary advice after the entire island population came down with a rash from eating so few fresh fruits and vegetables. Says Rigaud, "I ate more Popeye mullet and potatoes growing up. At school, the children would come with mullet fried in pig fat in brown paper sacks for their lunch." When he was in the 7th grade, he stopped school to go trawling after his father got sick. He says he was 20 years old before he first saw electricity, adding philosophically, "What you don't have you don't miss, and what you don't know won't hurt you."

During World War II, with rationing and shortages, times were still hard on the island. There were blackouts, even though there was no electricity, and no one would ever forget the torpedoing of the oil tank at Fourchon. Afterward the Coast Guard patrolled the lanes with dogs. Rigaud says there was no game warden then, nor was one needed. People killed plenty of marsh hens, but only as many as they needed; they didn't kill what they couldn't eat.

However tough times were, though, the people of Grand Isle shared what little they had and socialized with their neighbors, trading and helping each other according to an unspoken code of ethics, and they still do. Boaters to this day tell stories of being stranded offshore in stormy weather with stalled boat motors and getting towed to shore by island boys in small boats braving the pelting rains and lightning, refusing to accept any payment for their help.

After the war, Rigaud says,

> Things blew up like an atomic bomb, and the money and good times started rolling. The weekends were crowded, even though there was still just a gravel road, and there were barrooms and casinos, restaurants and whorehouses, movies.

It's gonna eventually get a little worse [Rigaud frets]. Recently I fixed the lock on my door, but for years I didn't even know where the keys to the house were, and 90 percent of the time my truck keys were in my truck. I hate to see retirees coming in and starting to tell us how to do [things]. I don't know how to say what I'm gonna say, but I don't think people enjoy life today like they used to. I learned to appreciate what little I got. We don't have all the conveniences—no McDonald's or Popeye's—but Grand Isle is a wonderful place to live if you want to go to bed at night without worrying.

Adds Raleigh Lasseigne, "Heaven, eh? Heaven, heaven." And he goes back home content to sit in his porch swing. And at peace with the world, he swings.

Raleigh's wife, Kay, provides some favorite recipes here. The Cho-Lo-Lo, a typical old Grand Isle dish, comes from the wonderful Web site of Galliano resident Janis Nihart, at www. geocities.com/Tokyo/Flats/4396/main2.html. She says she made the Web site when she saw how quickly life was changing. The Grand Isle she knew even as a child in the '50s and '60s no longer existed, and the Web site was the only way she knew to preserve it.

Stuffed Crabs

5 cups diced celery
2 large onions, diced
5 cups diced bell pepper
1 loaf French bread
4 lb. crabmeat, dark (claw meat) and white
1 bunch green onions, chopped
2 tsp. salt
1 tbsp. garlic powder
3 sticks butter
2-3 eggs
Breadcrumbs
Lemon juice, optional

Mix together celery, onions, and bell peppers and boil until tender, about 30 minutes. Drain in colander. Soften bread by soaking in water, squeezing out liquid, and draining well. In a large bowl combine bread and crabmeat very gently, folding crab in so meat does not break apart. Add green onions and boiled vegetables to softened bread. Drain any liquid from this mixture. Add seasonings. Sauté mixture a third at a time, using a stick of butter with each of the 3 portions. Cool. Whisk eggs and add to mixture to hold ingredients together. To form cakes, use ⅓ cup measure, fill with mixture, and turn onto cookie sheet covered with breadcrumbs. After making 36 mounds, shake breadcrumbs on top of each mound and then form into cakes. Deep-fry until golden. You may instead fry in skillet in peanut oil about 5 minutes on each side until golden, or bake at 400 degrees until browned. Top with a little lemon juice and pat of butter before cooking. Makes 36 crab cakes to serve 18.
Recipe from Kay Lasseigne.

Smothered Squid

2 lb. squid, cut into pieces or whole (for larger squid, use only tentacles)
8 onions, sliced
Oil
1 cup water

Wash squid well and remove membrane. Remove one eye at a time with a small knife, then flip squid over and remove the ink sac. The body of the squid is like a tube; gently slice one side and remove the transparent quill, a plastic-like, stiff membrane. Some people call the quill a feather or a shrimp. Flush squid with clean water and pat dry with paper towels. Drain on paper towels until ready to cook. Smother onions in oil, and cook down until tender. Add cleaned squid and water. The seafood will make some liquid, too. Simmer until tender, about 40-60 minutes, just like cooking smothered liver and onions. For small squid the entire body can be cooked, though the tentacles are the best part. Serves 10-12.
Recipe from Kay Lasseigne.

Cho-Lo-Lo

4 large onions, chopped
2 medium bell peppers, chopped
4 cloves garlic, chopped
½ cup cooking oil
1 cup water
¼-½ cup chopped parsley
1½ pt. fresh oysters

Brown onions, bell peppers, and garlic in oil. Add 1 cup water. Cook until thick. Add parsley and oysters, and cook about 15 minutes. Serves 4.
Recipe from Janis Vizier Nihart.

Port Fourchon

Port Fourchon, near Grand Isle, is home to a large fleet of deep-sea charter fishing boats. It is also a bustling oil and gas port right on the gulf at the southernmost point of Louisiana. The port supplies 75 percent of the Gulf of Mexico deepwater oil and gas drilling and some 18 percent of the oil and gas production for the entire nation. More than 600 oil platforms are within 40 miles of the port. It also services the Louisiana Offshore Oil Port (LOOP) unloading and distribution point for oil supertankers entering the gulf.

Louisiana's oil and gas industry is big, big, big. A thousand trucks a day are said to come and go from Port Fourchon, carrying workers and supplies. Old LA 1 has for years been the only overland route to the port, which is critical to the gulf's drilling infrastructure. With 1.7 million barrels of oil coursing through pipelines under Port Fourchon every day, port authorities for many years have pleaded for government funding for an elevated access highway, citing the disastrous effect on the nation's oil supply as well as the cost of gas in the event LA 1 should be wiped out by a direct hit from a strong hurricane sweeping swiftly out of the gulf and swamping the roadbed. Finally, in 2005, federal funds were loaned to the state to jumpstart construction of an elevated toll highway connecting Leeville to Port Fourchon, including a new 73-foot-high bridge over Bayou Lafourche at Leeville on LA 1 to replace a rickety 1970 lift bridge. Eventually the elevated highway will extend north of Leeville to Golden Meadow in an ambitious project expected to cost more than $550 million.

A big percentage of the population of south Louisiana works for, or has worked for, the oil and gas industry. That means, of course, that a huge percentage of men and women comprising the oil industry personnel are good old south Louisiana cooks. In addition, many of the country's top Louisiana-bred chefs got their earliest training right there on the offshore oil rigs, where the crews can be as demanding as in any fine dining establishment on land.

What could be more natural, then, than Patrick Walsh's *Oil and Gastronomy,* called the number-one oilfield cookbook and possibly the only one to have recognized the unlikely connection between these two energy sources, food and fossil fuel. Scattered throughout the book are illustrations and humorous explanations of the terminology and tools unique to the oil patch: roughnecks, pushers, jughustlers, mullets, knuckle joints, gumbo mud, idiot clips, doglegs, and pig traps. The recipes themselves represent some of the best of south Louisiana bayou cooking, and here are a few. To order *Oil and Gastronomy,* contact Patrick Walsh by mail at P.O. Box 1369, St. Francisville, LA 70775, by telephone at 225-635-6502, or online at pat@stfrancisvilleinn.com.

Cajun Cayenne Toast

2-3 loaves French bread
1 cup olive oil
2½ tsp. red cayenne pepper
1½ tsp. sugar
1½ tsp. salt
1½ tsp. onion powder
1½ tsp. garlic powder
1 tsp. paprika
½ tsp. ground black pepper

Using an electric knife, slice bread about ¼" thick. Spread slices in single layers on ungreased cookie sheets. Mix oil and all seasonings in a small bowl. Lightly coat one side of each bread slice. Whisk mixture often so seasonings will not settle to the bottom. In a 200-degree oven, dry slices until very crisp, similar to Melba toast. Cooking time should be approximately 1 hour. Best served fresh, but will keep several days. Also can be frozen. Serves 10-20.

Crab-Corn Soup

½ cup butter
1 onion, chopped
1 garlic clove, chopped
¼ cup flour
2 cups chicken stock or canned broth
2 cups fish stock or 2 bottles clam juice
1½ cups corn
1 tsp. salt
¼ tsp. black pepper
¼ tsp. cayenne pepper
⅛ tsp. thyme
2 cups whipping cream
1 lb. lump crabmeat, clean of shells
Shallots, chopped

In a soup pot, melt butter and add onion and garlic. Sauté until transparent and browning on the edges. Add flour. Stirring well, cook for 5 minutes. Add both stocks and bring to boil. Once thickened, lower heat to medium. Add corn. Add seasonings. Cook uncovered for 30 minutes. Add whipping cream and cook for 10 minutes, stirring constantly. Add crab and shallots in amount preferred and cook for 5 minutes. Serve in individual bowls and garnish with pinch of shallots on top. Serves 6-8.

Stuffed Flounder

½ stick butter
½ cup chopped onions
½ cup chopped celery
¼ cup chopped green pepper
⅓ cup chopped green onions
2 cloves garlic, minced
1 tbsp. flour
½ cup milk
½ cup dry white wine
½ lb. crabmeat
½ lb. cooked shrimp, peeled and chopped
1 egg, beaten
½ cup breadcrumbs
2 tbsp. parsley
Cayenne pepper to taste
Black pepper to taste
Salt to taste
1 3-lb. flounder
¼ cup melted

In butter, sauté onions, celery, green pepper, green onions, and garlic until tender. Stir in flour. Add milk and wine, and stir and cook until thickened. Remove from heat and add crabmeat, shrimp, egg, breadcrumbs, and parsley. Stir well and season to taste. Stuff flounder, closing edges with toothpicks. Place fish in a greased baking dish and brush fish with melted butter. Bake in 375-degree oven for approximately 25-30 minutes. Fish should be flaky. Serves 4-6.

After Sex Pie

2 pt. vanilla ice cream
1 chocolate wafer crust
10 Andes chocolate crème de menthe mints, cut into bite-size pieces
10 chocolate nonpareils, cut into chunks
5 chocolate-covered graham crackers, cut into bite-size pieces
1 Snickers bar, cut into bite-size pieces
1 Golden Almond chocolate bar, cut into bite-size pieces
1 dark chocolate bar, cut into bite-size pieces
½ cup butterscotch ice cream topping
⅓ cup chopped pecans
Soft whipped cream to garnish
1 strawberry

Spread 1 pt. ice cream over crust. Top with half the chocolate candies, chocolate-covered graham crackers, and candy bars. Using a large serving spoon or ice cream scoop, spoon remaining ice cream over top. Freeze at least 3 hours or overnight. Before serving, pour on butterscotch topping and sprinkle with pecans, remaining chocolate-covered graham crackers, and candy. Refrigerate about 10 minutes to soften ice cream slightly. Garnish with whipped cream and strawberry. This pie is excellent after sex, the recipe promises, as the chocolate quickly replenishes all that lost energy, and if you're out on the oil rigs with no partner handy, what the heck, eat the pie and you'll never miss the sex. Well, maybe.

Photo Index

～🌺～

St. Joseph Plantation: Front of house (p. 64). Rear of house (p. 65). Live oak tree (p. 66): photos courtesy St. Joseph Plantation. Cabin (pp. 67-68). Interior bathing room walls of *briquette-entre-poteaux* (p. 69). Side view of front of house (p. 71): photos by author. Cattle drive (p. 72): photo from Historic Lafourche Parish Collection, Archives and Special Collections, Nicholls State University, Thibodaux, LA, courtesy LA Department of Wildlife and Fisheries.

Madewood Plantation: Eugene Robinson's Floating Palace on Bayou Lafourche at the Madewood Landing, 1890 (p. 73): postcard courtesy Madewood. Christ Church in Napoleonville, built 1835 with several Pughs on its first vestry (p. 74). Col. Thomas Pugh and wife, Eliza Foley, c. 1848 (p. 74). 1885 rear view of Madewood (p. 74): photos courtesy William L. Martin Collection, Archives and Special Collections, Nicholls State University, Thibodaux, LA. Madewood home (pp. 75-76): photos by author.

The Edward Douglass White House: House photos (pp. 77-78): photos by author. Gov. E. D. White, 1793-1847 (p. 79): courtesy William L. Martin Collection, Archives and Special Collections, Nicholls State University, Thibodaux, LA.

Naquin's Bed & Breakfast: Alligators (pp. 82-84): photos courtesy Joyce Naquin. St. John's Episcopal Church (p. 85): photo by author. Jackson Street in Thibodaux with 3-mule cart and peddling wagon, old Schneider Saloon, and arc light hanging in middle of street, 1902 (p. 88): photo courtesy William L. Martin Collection, Archives and Special Collections, Nicholls State University, Thibodaux, LA.

Laurel Valley Plantation: Ruins of sugar mill (p. 89). Cabinscape across water (p. 90): photos courtesy Joyce Naquin. Quarters cabins (pp. 90-91). Laurel Valley store (p. 91). Ruins of sugar mill (p. 92). Store exhibits (pp. 93-95): photos by author.

Rienzi Plantation: Rienzi home (p. 96): photo by author.

Wetlands Acadian Cultural Center: Laurel Valley slave quarters (p. 100). Bayou Lafourche (p. 101): photos by author. Coffin in pirogue (p. 101). Palmetto-thatched house (p. 102). Denizens of the cheniere (pp. 102-3):

photos courtesy Thaddeus I. St. Martin Collection, Archives and Special Collections, Nicholls State University, Thibodaux.

The Culinary Herpetologist: Dr. Ernest Liner and his 45-pound lizard, Buster (p. 106): photo courtesy Matt Stamey, *Houma Courier*.

The Houma Indians of Bayou Country: Indian mass in Dulac (pp. 109-10): photos courtesy Joyce Naquin. Indian baskets, Ardoyne collection (111): photo by author. Pirogue with coffin on way to cemetery (p. 112): photo courtesy Thaddeus I. St. Martin Collection, Archives and Special Collections, Nicholls State University, Thibodaux, LA. Houma tribe with palmetto-thatched dwellings (p. 112): photos courtesy Brenda Dardar Robichaux, Tribal Chairwoman.

Historic Southdown Plantation: Southdown home (pp. 113-14): photos by author. Katharine Minor Pipes Butler, last generation of Minor family children to live in the Southdown House, in costume at age 4 as Tom Thumb's bride (p. 117): photo from author's collection.

The Minors of Southdown: Mary Minor in white dress (p. 118). Katharine Lintot Minor in black (pp. 120, 122): photos from author's collection.

Magnolia Plantation: Magnolia home (p. 123): photo by author. John Jackson Shaffer, Jr., and his wife and two children (p. 124). 1918 photo of Capt. John Jackson Shaffer, John Dalton Shaffer, John Jackson Shaffer, Jr., and their wives and children (p. 125): photos courtesy Lee Shaffer.

Magical Storybook Ardoyne: Ardoyne home (pp. 126-27). Washington portrait (p. 127). Collection of Indian baskets (p. 128). Half-hogshead in Ardoyne (p. 128): photos by author. Four generations of Shaffer family (p. 128). Margaret Krumbhaar Shaffer and her daughter Margaret (p. 129). Young Margaret K. Shaffer with olive jar at Southdown Plantation (p. 129): photos courtesy Margaret Shaffer.

Molasses: Sugarcane field with tractor (p. 130): photo courtesy Joyce Naquin. Cane cutting (p. 131). Sugarcane field water cart (p. 131). Sugar mill at Georgia Plantation, the old Mathews place (p. 132): photos courtesy William L. Martin Collection, Archives and Special Collections, Nicholls State University, Thibodaux, LA.

Dat Damn Nutr'a Rat: Nutria (p. 134): photo courtesy Louisiana Department of Wildlife and Fisheries. Egret (p. 135): photo courtesy Pat Walsh. Trapping photos (pp. 135-38, 140-41): from Historic Lafourche Parish Collection, Archives and Special Collections, Nicholls State University, Thibodaux, LA, courtesy LA Department of Wildlife and Fisheries.

Foret's Fine French Foods: Aline Foret (pp. 142, 144, 147): courtesy Aline Foret.

Oysters: Blessing of the fleet on Boudreaux Canal (p. 148). Gentlemen visitors on the drying platforms (p. 149): photos courtesy Thaddeus I. St. Martin Collection, Archives and Special Collections, Nicholls State University, Thibodaux, LA. Houma Indian Whitney Dardar shucking oysters (p. 151): photo courtesy Brenda Dardar Robichaux, Tribal Chairwoman. Fishermen in boat, old Grand Isle (p. 153): photo courtesy Raleigh and Kay Lasseigne. Oysterman with gas can. Oysterman in boat (p. 153): photos from Historic Lafourche Parish Collections, Archives and Special Collections, Nicholls State University, Thibodaux, LA, courtesy LA Department of Wildlife and Fisheries.

Shrimp Boats A'Coming: Shrimp boats (pp. 154-55). Estay Shrimp Company (p. 155): photos by author. Manila Village shrimp-drying platform (p. 156): photo courtesy Historic Lafourche Parish Collection; Shrimp platform (pp. 157-59): photos

courtesy Thaddeus I. St. Martin Collection, Archives and Special Collections, Nicholls State University, Thibodaux, LA.

Louisiana's Vanishing Coastline: Woodduck (p. 165). Flying waterfowl (p. 166). Hunter with dog (p. 167): photos courtesy Julia Sims, reprinted from *Vanishing Paradise*.

Grand Isle and Louisiana's Coastal Islands: Champion fisherman Terry St. Cyr (pp. 170-71): photos courtesy Terry St. Cyr. Smitty's Casino (p. 172). Bridge to Grand Isle, 1932 (p. 173): photos courtesy Raleigh and Kay Lasseigne.

Old Grand Isle: Crabber Raleigh Lasseigne in his porch swing (p. 178): photo by author. Chinatown fish-drying operation on Grand Isle (p. 179): photo courtesy Thaddeus I. St. Martin collection, Archives and Special Collections, Nicholls State University, Thibodaux, LA. Horse cart on beach (p. 180). Early taxi (p. 181). Farming cucumbers (p. 183). Covering plants to protect from cold (p. 183): photos courtesy Raleigh and Kay Lasseigne.

Port Fourchon: Early bayou swimmers off pier (p. 184): photo courtesy Thaddeus I. St. Martin Collection, Archives and Special Collections, Nicholls State University, Thibodaux, LA. Pelicans with oil platform in background (p. 185): photo courtesy Pat Walsh. Pelican (p. 187): photo from Historic Lafourche Parish Collection, Archives and Special Collections, Nicholls State University, Thibodaux, LA, courtesy LA Department of Wildlife and Fisheries.

Index